SIGN RE
(signs used in the

CW00662360

Good footpath - - -
(sufficiently distinct to

Intermittent footpath - - - - - - - - - -
(difficult to follow in mist)

Route recommended
    but no path ......>..................>....
(if recommended one way only, arrow indicates direction)

Wall ∞∞∞∞∞∞∞∞∞   Broken wall ∘∘∘∘∘∘∘∘∘∘∘∘∘

Fence ┼┼┼┼┼┼┼┼┼   Broken fence ιιιιιιιιιιιιιιιιιι

Marshy ground ⌄⌄⌄⌄⌄   Trees 🌳🌳🌳🌳

Crags 🏔🏔🏔   Boulders ▵▵▵▵

Stream or River
    (arrow indicates direction of flow)

Waterfall   Bridge

Buildings ▪▪▪   Unenclosed road ::::::::::::::::

Contours (at 100' intervals)
      1900
      1800
      1700

Summit-cairn ▲   Other (prominent) cairns △

THE
EASTERN
FELLS

REVISED EDITIONS

PUBLISHER'S NOTE

Fell walking can be dangerous, especially
in wet, windy, foggy or icy conditions.
Please be sure to take sensible precautions
when out on the fells. As A. Wainwright himself
frequently wrote: use your common sense
and watch where you are putting your feet.

A PICTORIAL GUIDE
TO THE
LAKELAND FELLS
SECOND EDITION
REVISED BY CHRIS JESTY
being an illustrated account
of a study and exploration
of the mountains in the
English Lake District

by

AWainwright

BOOK ONE
THE EASTERN FELLS

Frances Lincoln Limited
4 Torriano Mews
Torriano Avenue
London NW5 2RZ
www.franceslincoln.com

First edition published by Henry Marshall, Kentmere, 1955
First published by Frances Lincoln 2003
Second (revised) edition published by Frances Lincoln 2005
Reprinted with minor corrections 2007

Printed and bound in China

A CIP catalogue for this book is
available from the British Library

ISBN 978 0 7112 2465 0

9 8 7 6 5

THIS REVISED AND UPDATED EDITION PUBLISHED BY
FRANCES LINCOLN, LONDON

FOREWORD
BY BETTY WAINWRIGHT

The Pictorial Guides have never before been revised,
for the reasons given by AW in his concluding remarks
to the third volume, *The Central Fells*, where he wrote
that by the time he had finished Book Seven, age
would prevent him undertaking the 'joyful task' of
revising the series himself. He went on to write:

> ... Substantially, of course, the books will be useful
> for many years to come, especially in the detail and
> description of the fell tops, while the views will remain
> unaltered for ever, assuming that falling satellites and
> other fancy gadgets of man's invention don't blow
> God's far worthier creations to bits. But, this dire
> possibility apart, the books must inevitably show
> more and more inaccuracies as the years go by.
> Therefore, because it is unlikely that there will ever
> be revised editions, and because I should just hate to
> see my name on anything that could not be relied
> on, the probability is that the books will progressively
> be withdrawn from publication after a currency of a
> few years.

This was written in 1958, when the oldest volume was
only three years old and by the time he had completed
Book Seven in 1965 he was even more conscious of the
little things that had gone out of date in the previous
volumes — cairns demolished or built, screes eroded,
woods felled or grown up, new paths made. As the
years passed and it became apparent that the books
were still in demand, despite these inaccuracies, he
was occasionally approached by people asking for
revised editions. But the core of the problem was that,
as old age approached, he knew he could not
undertake the changes himself, nor did he trust
anyone to do the work as he would have wished.
  When, in 1980, Chris Jesty broached the idea to him,
he was told 'after my lifetime'. This was half the
battle won — AW knew Chris's work well, and did trust
him. Now, given the continuing popularity and use of

the Pictorial Guides, I am delighted that, due to Chris's commitment, the guides are being revised and I give them my blessing. It is with pleasure that I picture Chris re-walking and checking and, where necessary, correcting every route, every ascent and every path. Although most of the individual corrections are minor, the overall impact is huge, and I feel proud and confident — as I am sure AW would be too — that the revised guides will satisfy the needs of the 21st-century walker.

Betty Wainwright
Kendal, January 2005

INTRODUCTION
TO THE
SECOND EDITION
BY CHRIS JESTY

In 1959 I went on an Outward Bound course at Eskdale Green, which involved a lot of walking in the mountains. I found that the depiction of paths on Ordnance Survey maps left definite room for improvement, and I had the idea of producing a guide book that would make it easier for people to find their way around. But in 1961 I was given one of Wainwright's Pictorial Guides to the Lakeland Fells and discovered that he had beaten me to it.

It occurred to me that one day the books would become out of date, and that, as I was presumably much younger than the author, the time might arrive when I would be allowed to revise them. It has taken more than forty years for that dream to turn into a reality.

In the meantime I had made the acquaintance of the author. I collaborated with him on *A Guide to the View from Scafell Pike*, and later on, when his eyesight was failing, I drew the maps for two of his other books (*Wainwright in the Limestone Dales* and *Wainwright's Favourite Lakeland Mountains*). Shortly before he died he requested that if ever the Lakeland Guides were to be revised I should be offered the job.

When, in 2003, following a change of publisher, the proposal was revived, I threw myself into the job with enthusiasm. I had a number of advantages over the author. I had a car, I had satellite navigation equipment, I was able to work on enlargements of the pages, and as I didn't have a job I was able to devote all my time and all my energy to this vast project.

Every feature on the maps and ascent diagrams and every word of text have been checked, but I have not checked every recommended route without a path. Descriptions of natural features and views are virtually unaltered, but the number of changes

INTRODUCTION TO THE SECOND EDITION

that have been made to maps and ascent diagrams is enormous. The decision was taken to print the paths in a second colour so that they stand out from other details, and also so that readers can tell at a glance that it is the revised edition they are using.

Summit altitudes have been corrected where they differ by five feet or more from the latest Ordnance Survey figures. Parking information has been added where appropriate. I have also taken the liberty of adding other information that seems to me to be of interest. No changes have been made to drawings of landscapes, natural features or buildings, or, of course, to Wainwright's 'Personal Notes in Conclusion'.

Occasional references will be found in the books to Bartholomew's maps. These are still available, but they are now published by Collins.

In order to keep the books as accurate as possible, and in anticipation of future revised editions, readers are invited to write to me (c/o the publishers) about any errors they find in the revised Pictorial Guides. Emails to chrisj@frances-lincoln.com and letters sent to me c/o Frances Lincoln, 4 Torriano Mews, Torriano Avenue, London NW5 2RZ, will be passed on regularly.

Chris Jesty
Kendal, January 2005

I should like to thank Ian Sager and Jeff Coates for drawing my attention to errors, which have now been corrected. Updates on changes that have taken place since publication are now available on the web page for this volume on the Frances Lincoln website (www.franceslincoln.com).

Chris Jesty
Kendal, January 2011

BOOK ONE

is dedicated to

THE MEN OF THE ORDNANCE SURVEY

whose maps of Lakeland
have given me much pleasure
both on the fells
and by my fireside

INTRODUCTION

INTRODUCTION

Surely there is no other place in this whole wonderful world quite like Lakeland ...no other so exquisitely lovely, no other so charming, no other that calls so insistently across a gulf of distance. All who truly love Lakeland are exiles when away from it.

Here, in small space, is the wonderland of childhood's dreams, lingering far beyond childhood through the span of a man's life: its enchantment grows with passing years and quiet eventide is enriched by the haunting sweetness of dear memories, memories that remain evergreen through the flight of time, that refresh and sustain in the darker days. How many, these memories...........the moment of wakening, and the sudden joyful realisation that this is to be another day of freedom on the hills .... the dawn chorus of bird-song .... the delicate lacework of birches against the sky ...... morning sun drawing aside the veils of mist; black-stockinged lambs, in springtime, amongst the daffodils......... silver cascades dancing and leaping down bracken steeps ..... autumn colours ....a red fox running over snow .... the silence of lonely hills ...... storm and tempest in the high places, and the unexpected glimpses of valleys dappled in sunlight far beneath the swirling clouds .... rain, and the intimate shelter of lichened walls .... fierce winds on the heights and soft breezes that are no more than gentle caresses ....a sheepdog watching its master

.... the snow and ice and freezing stillnesses of midwinter: a white world, rosy-pink as the sun goes down .... the supreme moment when the top cairn comes into sight at last, only minutes away, after the long climb .... the small ragged sheep that brave the blizzards .... the symphonies of murmuring streams, unending, with never a discord ...... curling smoke from the chimneys of the farm down below amongst the trees, where the day shall end ...... oil-lamps in flagged kitchens, huge fires in huge fireplaces, huge suppers .... glittering moonlight on placid waters ...... stars above dark peaks ..... the tranquillity that comes before sleep, when thoughts are of the day that is gone and the day that is to come .... All these memories, and so many more, breathing anew the rare quality and magical atmosphere of Lakeland ...... memories that belong to Lakeland, and could not belong in the same way to any other place .... memories that enslave the mind forever.

Many are they who have fallen under the spell of Lakeland, and many are they who have been moved to tell of their affection, in story and verse and picture and song.

This book is one man's way of expressing his devotion to Lakeland's friendly hills. It was conceived, and is born, after many years of inarticulate worshipping at their shrines.

It is, in very truth, a love-letter.

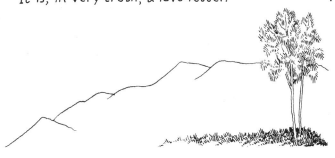

Classification and Definition

Any division of the Lakeland fells into geographical districts must necessarily be arbitrary, just as the location of the outer boundaries of Lakeland must always be a matter of opinion. Any attempt to define internal or external boundaries is certain to invite criticism, and he who takes it upon himself to say where Lakeland starts and finishes, or, for example, where the Central Fells merge into the Southern Fells and *which* fells *are* the Central Fells and which the Southern and *why* they need be so classified, must not expect his pronouncements to be generally accepted.

Yet for present purposes some plan of classification and definition must be used. County and parochial boundaries are no help, nor is the recently-defined area of the Lakeland National Park, for this book is concerned only with the high ground.

First, the external boundaries.   Straight lines linking the extremities of the outlying lakes enclose all the higher fells very conveniently. There are a few fells of lesser height to the north and east, however, that are typically Lakeland in character and cannot properly be omitted : these are brought in, somewhat untidily, by extending the lines in those areas. Thus:

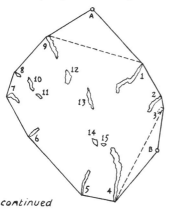

1 : *Ullswater*
2 : *Hawes Water*
3 : proposed *Swindale Resr*
4 : *Windermere*
5 : *Coniston Water*
6 : *Wast Water*
7 : *Ennerdale Water*
8 : *Loweswater*
9 : *Bassenthwaite Lake*
10 : *Crummock Water*
11 : *Buttermere*
12 : *Derwent Water*
13 : *Thirlmere*
14 : *Grasmere*
15 : *Rydal Water*
A : *Caldbeck*
B : Longsleddale (church)

continued

Classification and Definition

continued

The complete Guide includes all the fells in the area enclosed by the straight lines of the diagram. This is an undertaking quite beyond the compass of a single volume, and it is necessary, therefore, to divide the area into convenient sections, making the fullest use of natural boundaries (lakes, valleys and low passes) so that each district is, as far as possible, self-contained and independent of the rest.

This division gives seven areas, each with a well-defined group of fells, and each area is the subject of a separate volume

1 : The Eastern Fells
2 : The Far Eastern Fells
3 : The Central Fells
4 : The Southern Fells
5 : The Northern Fells
6 : The North-western Fells
7 : The Western Fells

INTRODUCTION

Notes on the Illustrations

THE MAPS .... Many excellent books have been written about Lakeland, but the best literature of all for the walker is that published by the Director General of Ordnance Survey, the 1" map for companionship and guidance on expeditions, the 2½" map for exploration both on the fells and by the fireside. These admirable maps are remarkably accurate topographically but there is a crying need for a revision of the paths on the hills: several walkers' tracks that have come into use during the past few decades, some of them now broad highways, are not shown at all; other paths still shown on the maps have fallen into neglect and can no longer be traced on the ground.

The popular Bartholomew 1" map is a beautiful picture, fit for a frame, but this too is unreliable for paths; indeed here the defect is much more serious, for routes are indicated where no paths ever existed, nor ever could — the cartographer has preferred to take precipices in his stride rather than deflect his graceful curves over easy ground.

Hence the justification for the maps in this book: they have the one merit (of importance to walkers) of being dependable as regards delineation of *paths*. They are intended as supplements to the Ordnance Survey maps, certainly not as substitutes.

THE VIEWS .... Various devices have been used to illustrate the views from the summits of the fells. The full panorama in the form of an outline drawing is most satisfactory generally, and this method has been adopted for the main viewpoints.

THE DIAGRAMS OF ASCENTS .... The routes of ascent of the higher fells are depicted by diagrams that do not pretend to strict accuracy: they are neither plans nor elevations; in fact there is deliberate distortion in order to show detail clearly: usually they are represented as viewed from imaginary 'space-stations.' But it is hoped they will be useful and interesting.

THE DRAWINGS .... The drawings at least are honest attempts to reproduce what the eye sees: they illustrate features of interest and also serve the dual purpose of breaking up the text and balancing the layout of the pages, and of filling up awkward blank spaces, like this:

Thirlmere

THE
EASTERN
FELLS

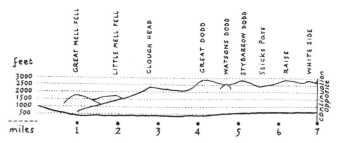

In the area of the Eastern Fells the greatest single mass of high ground in Lakeland is concentrated. It takes the form of a tremendous barrier running north and south, consistently high and steep throughout its length, mainly having an altitude between 2500'-3000', in two places only falling below 2000', and rising above 3000' on Helvellyn. In general the western slopes are steep, smooth and grassy and the eastern slopes are broken and craggy, but at the northern extremity the reverse obtains. The fells in this area may conveniently be classed in two groups divided by Grisedale Pass: in the south is the Fairfield group, pleasingly arrayed and with deep valleys cutting into the mass on both flanks; north is the bigger but less interesting Helvellyn range, with no valleys in the high western wall but several on the eastern side running down to Ullswater.

The geographical boundaries of the area are distinct. In shape it is a long inverted triangle, covering about fifty square miles of territory, based on Ambleside. The western boundary is formed by the deep trough of Dunmail Raise and Thirlmere, a great rift of which the principal road across the district takes advantage;

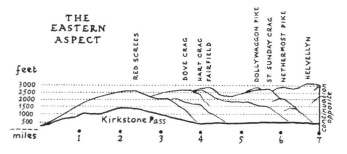

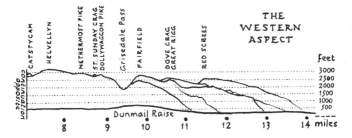

the eastern boundary is the trench of Kirkstone Pass
and Ullswater, and the northern is the broad Keswick
to Penrith gap. These boundaries are very satisfactory,
enclosing all the dependencies of Helvellyn and Fairfield,
and they are particularly convenient for the purposes
of a separate guidebook because they are not crossed,
normally, during the course of a day's fell-walk. Only
at Kirkstone is there a link with fells outside the area
but even here the breach is very pronounced.

This is an area easily accessible and (excepting the fells
north of Sticks Pass) much frequented by walkers. It has
in Helvellyn the most-often-climbed mountain in Lakeland
and in Grisedale Pass one of the best-known footpaths.

Ambleside and Grasmere are favourite resorts for those
who frequent these fells, but, because the most dramatic
features are invariably presented to the east, the quiet
and beautiful Patterdale valley is far superior as a base
for their exploration: the eastern approaches are more
interesting, the surroundings more charming and the
views more rewarding; furthermore, from Patterdale
any part of the main ridge may be visited in a normal
day's expedition.

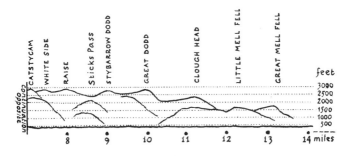

THE EASTERN FELLS

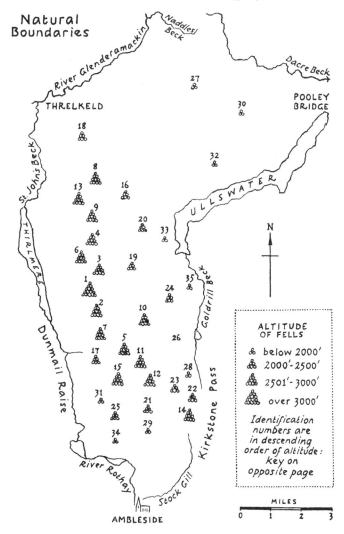

Natural
Boundaries

River Glenderamackin

Naddle(s) Beck

Dacre Beck

THRELKELD

POOLEY BRIDGE

St John's Beck

THIRLMERE

ULLSWATER

Dunmail Raise

Goldrill Beck

Kirkstone Pass

River Rothay

Stock Gill

AMBLESIDE

N

ALTITUDE
OF FELLS

🜄 below 2000'

🜂 2000'-2500'

🜃 2501'-3000'

🜁 over 3000'

Identification
numbers are
in descending
order of altitude:
key on
opposite page

MILES
0   1   2   3

THE EASTERN FELLS

in the order of
their appearance
in this book

over 3000'	2501'-3000'	2000'-2500'	below 2000'		Reference to map opposite		Altitude in feet
			35	..	ARNISON CRAG	..	1424
		19		..	BIRKHOUSE MOOR	..	2356
		24			BIRKS	..	2040
	3				CATSTYCAM		2917
		18			CLOUGH HEAD	..	2381
	7			..	DOLLYWAGGON PIKE	..	2815
	12			..	DOVE CRAG	..	2598
	5			..	FAIRFIELD	..	2863
			33	..	GLENRIDDING DODD	..	1450
			32	..	GOWBARROW FELL	..	1579
	8			..	GREAT DODD	..	2812
			27	..	GREAT MELL FELL	..	1760
	15			..	GREAT RIGG	..	2513
	11			..	HART CRAG	..	2698
		16		..	HART SIDE	..	2481
			26	..	HARTSOP ABOVE HOW	..	1870
1				..	HELVELLYN	..	3118
		25		..	HERON PIKE	..	2008
			28	..	HIGH HARTSOP DODD	..	1702
		21		..	HIGH PIKE	..	2155
		23		..	LITTLE HART CRAG	..	2091
			30	..	LITTLE MELL FELL	..	1657
			29	..	LOW PIKE	..	1667
		22		..	MIDDLE DODD	..	2146
			34	..	NAB SCAR	..	1450
	2			..	NETHERMOST PIKE	..	2920
	4			..	RAISE	..	2897
	14			..	RED SCREES	..	2546
	10			..	SAINT SUNDAY CRAG	..	2756
		17		..	SEAT SANDAL	..	2415
		20		..	SHEFFIELD PIKE	..	2215
			31	..	STONE ARTHUR	..	1652
	9			..	STYBARROW DODD	..	2770
	13			..	WATSON'S DODD	..	2589
	6			..	WHITE SIDE	..	2832
1	14	10	10				
		35					

Each fell is the subject
of a separate chapter

Arnison Crag 1424'

from Keldas

Glenridding

Patterdale

ARNISON CRAG ▲

BIRKS ▲

Sᵗ SUNDAY CRAG ▲

MILES
0   1   2

The rough fellside curving out of Deepdale and bounding the highway to Patterdale village has an attractive rocky crown, often visited for the fine view it offers of the head of Ullswater. This is Arnison Crag, a low hill with a summit worthy of a mountain. It is a dependency of Sᵗ Sunday Crag, forming the lesser of the two prongs which constitute the north-east spur of that grand fell; Birks is the other. It starts as a grass shelf east of Cold Cove and then takes the shape of a curving ridge of no particular interest except for the sudden upthrust of its craggy summit.

MAP

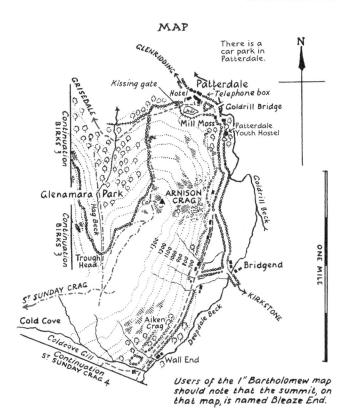

Users of the 1" Bartholomew map should note that the summit, on that map, is named Bleaze End.

ASCENT FROM PATTERDALE

The ascent is invariably made from the village of Patterdale. A lane leads up opposite the telephone box and bends right. After the bend, a path on the left skirts the attractive marshy area of Mill Moss. The old tin cans and motor tyres that were much in evidence here have been cleared away, and this is now a delightful spot. Go left at a T-junction and through a kissing gate. Then follow the wall of Glenamara Park up the hill. Stay on the path until you come to a col and then take a turning on the left. When this comes to an end, scramble up the rocks ahead. *Although a short and easy walk, the ascent may lead to difficulties in mist and should then not be attempted.*

THE SUMMIT

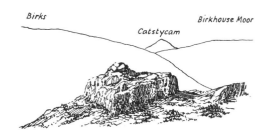

The summit is a rock platform, inaccessible to the walker on the west side and attained from other directions only by breaches in a low wall of crag defending it. A rock gateway (seen from the road near Hartsop as a clean-cut notch on the skyline) separates this platform from another at a slightly lower elevation which has the principal cairn and overlooks the approach from Patterdale.

The lower cairn (now collapsed)

The summit from the south

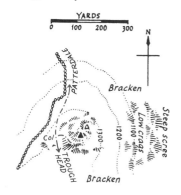

DESCENTS: The ridge should be followed down, for Patterdale. 'Short cuts' are likely to encounter rougher ground. A longer alternative follows the wall to Trough Head, where a very awkward stepstile gives access to the wooded Glenamara Park and pleasant paths which lead back to Patterdale.
‖ In mist, make a wide detour to the wall and follow it down northwards.

THE VIEW

Arnison Crag is surrounded by higher fells, and the view is very restricted. A feature is the fine grouping of the hills above the pastures of Hartsop.

Ullswater is the only lake seen, its upper reach being well displayed. This is not, however, the best viewpoint for Ullswater by any means.

Principal Fells

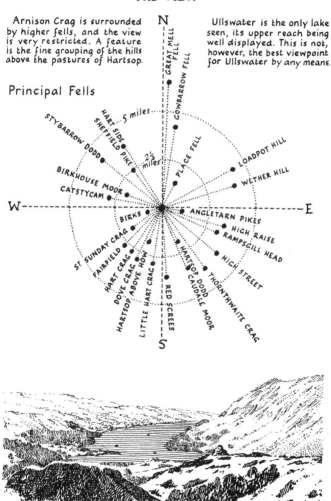

N

GREAT MELL FELL
GOWBARROW FELL
5 miles
STYBARROW DODD
HART SIDE
SHEFFIELD PIKE
2½ miles
PLACE FELL
LOADPOT HILL
WETHER HILL
BIRKHOUSE MOOR
CATSTYCAM
W
BIRKS
ANGLETARN PIKES
E
HIGH RAISE
RAMPSGILL HEAD
ST SUNDAY CRAG
FAIRFIELD
HART CRAG
DOVE CRAG
HARTSOP ABOVE HOW
LITTLE HART CRAG
HARTSOP DODD
CAUDALE MOOR
HIGH STREET
THORNTHWAITE CRAG
RED SCREES
S

Ullswater

Birkhouse Moor 2356'

from Lanty's Tarn

RAISE ▲   Glenridding ●
        BIRKHOUSE MOOR
        Patterdale ●
HELVELLYN ▲

▲ FAIRFIELD

MILES
0   1   2   3   4

NATURAL FEATURES

The east ridge of Helvellyn starts as a narrow rock arete, known to all walkers as *Striding Edge*, and then gradually widens into the broad sprawling mass of Birkhouse Moor. A long grassy promenade is the main characteristic of the top, but the southern slopes soon steepen to form a natural wall for Grisedale for two miles; this flank is traversed by one of the most popular paths in the district. Northwards, Red Tarn Beck and Glenridding Beck form its boundaries; there are crags on this side, mainly concentrated around the only defined ridge descending from the summit, north-east. The name 'moor' is well suited to this fell, the top particularly being grassy and dull; below, eastwards, there are patches of heather, and in this direction the fell ends abruptly and craggily above Ullswater, the lower slopes being beautifully wooded.

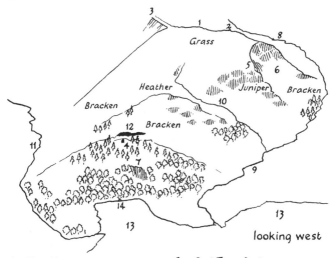

looking west

1 : *The highest point*	8 : *Red Tarn Beck*
2 : *The cairn at 2318'*	9 : *Glenridding Beck*
3 : *Ridge continuing to Helvellyn*	10 : *Mires Beck*
4 : *Keldas*	11 : *Grisedale Beck*
5 : *The north-east ridge*	12 : *Lanty's Tarn*
6 : *Blea Cove*	13 : *Ullswater*
7 : *Raven Crag*	14 : *St. Patrick's Well*

MAP

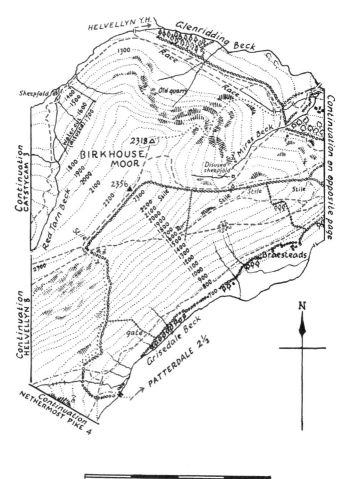

ONE MILE

MAP

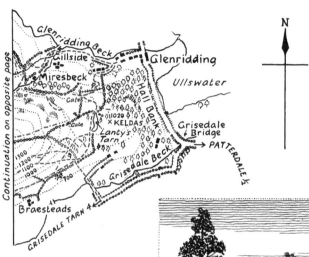

ONE MILE

Continuation on opposite page

KELDAS ——

Birkhouse Moor falls away to the east in bracken-clad slopes, but its extremity is an abrupt wooded height overlooking the upper reach of Ullswater. The pines here are a joy to behold, framing very beautiful views of the nearby lake and fells. The summit is accessible from Lanty's Tarn, but the eastern face is very steep and craggy. Artists and photographers will vote Keldas the loveliest and most delightful place amongst the eastern fells.

Ullswater from Keldas

ASCENT FROM GRISEDALE
1900 feet of ascent : 3½ miles from Patterdale village

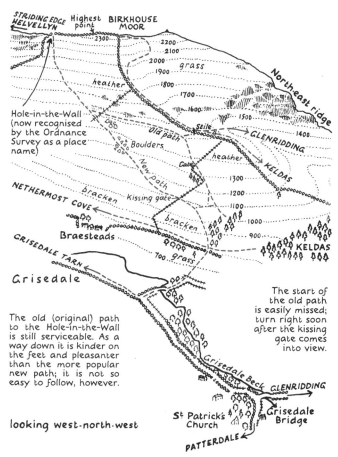

STRIDING EDGE
HELVELLYN
Highest point
BIRKHOUSE MOOR
2300
2200
2100
2000
1900
1800
1700
1600
1500
1400
grass
heather
North east ridge

Hole-in-the-Wall (now recognised by the Ordnance Survey as a place name)

Old path
Boulders
New path
Stile
GLENRIDDING
Gate
heather
KELDAS
1300
1200
1100

NETHERMOST COVE
bracken
Kissing gate
bracken
1000
900
KELDAS

Braesteads
700 grass

GRISEDALE TARN

Grisedale

The old (original) path to the Hole-in-the-Wall is still serviceable. As a way down it is kinder on the feet and pleasanter than the more popular new path; it is not so easy to follow, however.

The start of the old path is easily missed; turn right soon after the kissing gate comes into view.

Grisedale Beck
GLENRIDDING
Grisedale Bridge
St Patrick's Church
PATTERDALE

looking west-north-west

Birkhouse Moor may most easily be ascended by using the well-defined Patterdale-Striding Edge path climbing across its flank. The splendid views of Grisedale are the chief merit of this route, which is safe in bad conditions.

ASCENT FROM GLENRIDDING
1900 feet of ascent : 2 miles

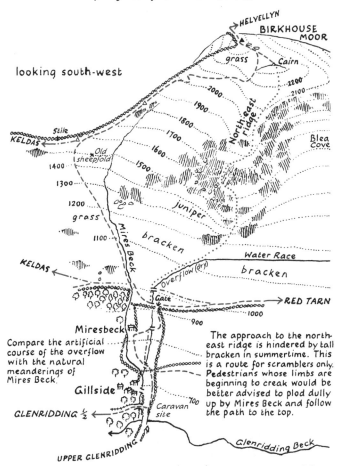

The approach to the north-east ridge is hindered by tall bracken in summertime. This is a route for scramblers only. Pedestrians whose limbs are beginning to creak would be better advised to plod dully up by Mires Beck and follow the path to the top.

Compare the artificial course of the overflow with the natural meanderings of Mires Beck.

The north-east ridge offers a mild adventure and is a test in route-finding amongst low crags. It is the best way up, with a beautiful view in retrospect, but in bad weather the Mires Beck route is preferable, and safer.

THE SUMMIT

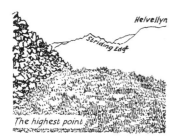

The highest point

The cairn at 2318'

The top can be reached easily and quickly from the popular Striding Edge path, but the detour is not really worth making. A few small tarns relieve the monotony of the grassy expanse, but generally the summit is without interest. A cairn indicates what appears to be the natural summit, but the prominent wall actually passes over higher ground marked by a second cairn.

North-east ridge

2318

Small tarns

Grass

N

HELVELLYN 2100 2200 2100 2000

GLENRIDDING

YARDS

0 100 200 300

The summit of Keldas as it appeared in 1954

DESCENTS: The descent is best made by following the new path to the saddle above Mires Beck: here turn left for Glenridding, or (for Patterdale) cross the wall at the stile to join a path going down to the right. The north-east ridge is not suitable for descent.

In bad weather conditions follow the path down to Glenridding. Avoid the east and north faces.

THE VIEW

The east face of Helvellyn, enclosed between the twin arms of Striding Edge and Swirral Edge, is the best feature of a rather dull panorama.

Lakes and Tarns
N : *Sticks Res.* (dry)
NE : *Ullswater* (better seen from the cairn at 2318)
ESE : *Angle Tarn*
SE : *Hayes Water*
S : *Grisedale Tarn*
WNW : *Keppelcove Tarn* (dry)

Principal Fells
(from the highest point)

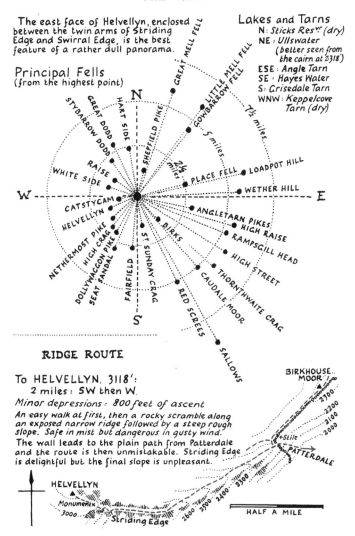

RIDGE ROUTE

To HELVELLYN, 3118':
2 miles : SW then W.

Minor depressions : 800 feet of ascent

An easy walk at first, then a rocky scramble along an exposed narrow ridge followed by a steep rough slope. Safe in mist but dangerous in gusty wind. The wall leads to the plain path from Patterdale and the route is then unmistakable. Striding Edge is delightful but the final slope is unpleasant.

HALF A MILE

Birks

2040'

Glenridding

Patterdale

ARNISON CRAG ▲

BIRKS ▲

St SUNDAY CRAG
▲

MILES

0   1   2

from Ullswater

The north-east shoulder of St Sunday Crag falls sharply to a depression beyond which a grassy undulating spur, featureless and wide, continues with little change in elevation towards Ullswater before finally plunging down to the valley through the enclosure of Glenamara Park. Although this spur lacks a distinctive summit it is sufficiently well-defined to deserve a separate name; but, being an unromantic and uninteresting fell, it has earned for itself nothing better than the prosaic and unassuming title of Birks. It is rarely visited as the sole objective of an expedition, but walkers descending the ridge from St Sunday Crag often take it in their stride.

NATURAL FEATURES

Above the 1900' contour Birks is a half-mile's easy grass promenade and there is nothing here to suggest that there are formidable crags below on both sides. Yet the Grisedale flank has a continuous line of cliffs and round to the east are several tiers of rock above the lower wooded slopes of Glenamara Park. Beyond the hollow of Trough Head, where rises Birks' only stream of note, is a curving ridge which culminates in the rocky pyramid of Arnison Crag; both this lower ridge and Birks itself, together forming a high wedge of rough ground between Grisedale and Deepdale, are dependencies of St Sunday Crag, Birks especially being dominated by this fine mountain.

looking south-west

1: The summit
2: Ridge continuing to St Sunday Crag
3: Black Crag
4: Harrison Crag
5: Birks Crag
6: Elmhow Crag
7: Thornhow End
8: Glenamara Park
9: Trough Head
10: Cold Cove Gill
11: Grisedale Beck
12: Hag Beck

Ullswater from Thornhow End

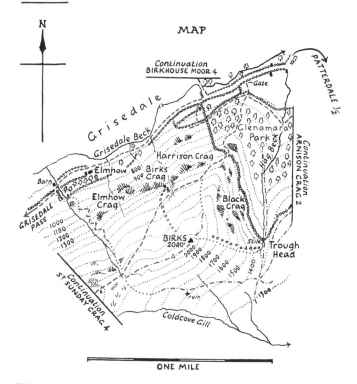

N

MAP

PATTERDALE ½

Continuation
BIRKHOUSE MOOR 4

Gate

G r i s e d a l e

Grisedale Beck

Glenamara
Park

Continuation
ARNISON CRAG 2

Hag Beck

Harrison Crag

Barn

Elmhow

Birks
Crag

Elmhow
Crag

GRISEDALE PASS

Black
Crag

BIRKS
2040

2000
1900
1800
1700

Stile

Trough
Head

Continuation
ST SUNDAY CRAG 4

1000
1100
1200
1300

ruin

1600
1500
1400

1900

Coldcove Gill

ONE MILE

Place Fell from Glenamara Park

ASCENTS FROM PATTERDALE
1600 feet of ascent : 2½ miles (1¾ by short variations)

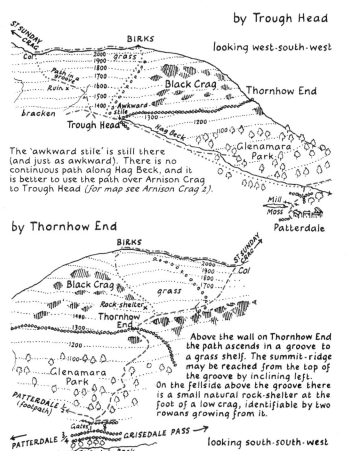

by Trough Head

looking west-south-west

The 'awkward stile' is still there (and just as awkward). There is no continuous path along Hag Beck, and it is better to use the path over Arnison Crag to Trough Head *(for map see Arnison Crag 2)*.

by Thornhow End

Above the wall on Thornhow End the path ascends in a groove to a grass shelf. The summit-ridge may be reached from the top of the groove by inclining left.
On the fellside above the groove there is a small natural rock-shelter at the foot of a low crag, identifiable by two rowans growing from it.

looking south-south-west

The Thornhow End path is very attractive, with glorious views, but it is steep. The Trough Head route is without a path in places and is uninteresting. There is no pleasure, and some danger, in climbing Birks in misty conditions.

THE SUMMIT

The summit has no interesting features. Do not believe out-of-date Ordnance Survey maps that promised a beacon here: all that can be found is an insignificant mound of stones almost obscured by grass. A more considerable heap of bigger stones further along the ridge appears to be a collapsed edifice of some kind.

There is a narrow track along the crest to the west of the summit.

DESCENTS: The finest way down (because of the view of Ullswater) is by the ridge to the north, inclining left to the path on the grass shelf below to avoid steep rough ground at the end of the ridge.

▌▌▌ *In bad weather conditions*, search eastwards for the top of the ▌▌▌ broken wall and follow it down to Trough Head.

RIDGE ROUTE

To ST SUNDAY CRAG
2756': 1¼ miles : SW
Minor depressions
800 feet of ascent

An easy stroll on grass to the col is followed by steep climbing up the ridge to the sloping summit-plateau; the alternative path (left) is easier. *Not recommended in mist.*

ONE MILE

THE VIEW

This is a scene of strong contrasts, interesting and pleasing but not extensive.

Principal Fells

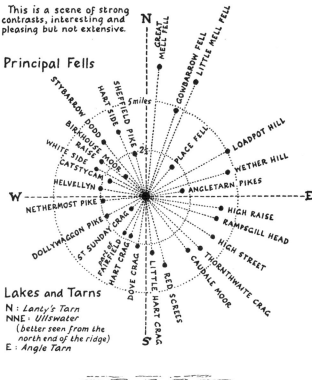

N

GREAT MELL FELL
GOWBARROW FELL
LITTLE MELL FELL
STYBARROW DODD
HART SIDE
SHEFFIELD PIKE
BIRKHOUSE MOOR
RAISE
WHITE SIDE
CATSTYCAM
HELVELLYN
NETHERMOST PIKE
DOLLYWAGGON PIKE
ST SUNDAY CRAG
part of FAIRFIELD
HART CRAG
DOVE CRAG
LITTLE HART CRAG
RED SCREES
CAUDALE MOOR
THORNTHWAITE CRAG
HIGH STREET
RAMPSGILL HEAD
HIGH RAISE
ANGLETARN PIKES
WETHER HILL
LOADPOT HILL
PLACE FELL

5 miles

W — — — — — **E**

S

Lakes and Tarns

N : *Lanty's Tarn*
NNE : *Ullswater*
(better seen from the north end of the ridge)
E : *Angle Tarn*

Ullswater

Catstycam

2917'

sometimes called
Catchedicam or
Catstye Cam

from Glenridding Beck

RAISE
▲

Glenridding
●

CATSTYCAM
▲

Patterdale
●

HELVELLYN
▲

MILES

0   1   2   3   4

NATURAL FEATURES

If Catstycam stood alone, remote from its fellows, it would be one of the finest peaks in Lakeland. It has nearly, but not quite, the perfect mountain form, with true simplicity in its soaring lines, and a small pointed top, a real summit, that falls away sharply on all sides. From Birkhouse Moor especially it has the appearance of a symmetrical pyramid; and from the upper valley of Glenridding it towers into the sky most impressively. But when seen from other directions it is too obviously dominated by Helvellyn and although its sharp peaked top identifies it unmistakably in every view in which it appears, clearly it is no more than the abrupt terminus of a short spur of the higher mountain, to which it is connected by a fine rock ridge, Swirral Edge. Its best feature is the tremendous shattered face it presents to the valley to the north, riven by a great scree gully. The steep slopes are nearly dry, but there is marshy ground around the base; the waters from Catstycam drain into Red Tarn Beck and Glenridding Beck.

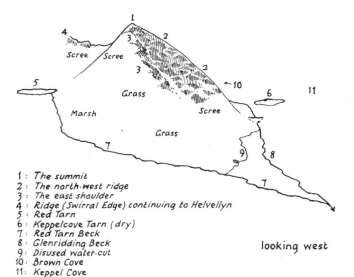

1 : The summit
2 : The north-west ridge
3 : The east shoulder
4 : Ridge (Swirral Edge) continuing to Helvellyn
5 : Red Tarn
6 : Keppelcove Tarn (dry)
7 : Red Tarn Beck
8 : Glenridding Beck
9 : Disused water-cut
10 : Brown Cove
11 : Keppel Cove

looking west

MAP

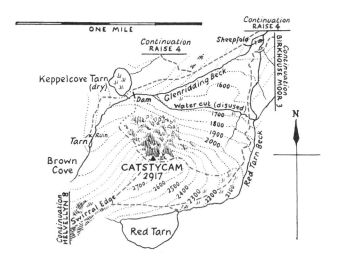

ONE MILE

Continuation
RAISE 4

Continuation
RAISE 4

Sheepfold

Continuation
BIRKHOUSE MOOR 3

Keppelcove Tarn
(dry)

Dam

Glenridding Beck

1600

Water cut (disused)

1700

Tarn   Ruin

1800
1900
2000

Brown
Cove

CATSTYCAM
2917

2700 2600 2500 2400 2300 2200 2100

Red Tarn Beck

Continuation
HELVELLYN 8

Swirral Edge

Red Tarn

N

Helvellyn and Swirral Edge

ASCENT FROM GLENRIDDING
2500 feet of ascent : 4 miles from Glenridding village

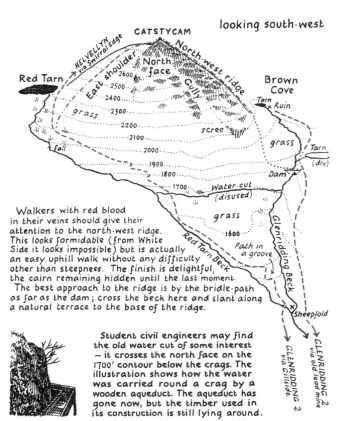

looking south-west

CATSTYCAM

HELVELLYN via Swirral Edge

North-west ridge

Red Tarn

East shoulder

North face

2600

Brown Cove

2500

Tarn
× Ruin

2400

grass

2300

Gully

2200

2100

scree

grass

Tarn (dry)

2000

Fall

1900

1800

Dam

1700

Water cut (disused)

Walkers with red blood
in their veins should give their
attention to the north-west ridge.
This looks formidable (from White
Side it looks impossible) but is actually
an easy uphill walk without any difficulty
other than steepness. The finish is delightful,
the cairn remaining hidden until the last moment.
  The best approach to the ridge is by the bridle-path
as far as the dam; cross the beck here and slant along
a natural terrace to the base of the ridge.

grass

1600

Red Tarn Beck

Path in a groove

Glenridding Beck

× Sheepfold

GLENRIDDING 2 via Gillside

GLENRIDDING 2 via old lead mine

Student civil engineers may find
the old water cut of some interest
— it crosses the north face on the
1700' contour below the crags. The
illustration shows how the water
was carried round a crag by a
wooden aqueduct. The aqueduct has
gone now, but the timber used in
its construction is still lying around.

Of the two routes shown, that by Red Tarn Beck and the
east shoulder is easy, on grass all the way. The north-west
ridge is steep and stony but a good airy climb in its later
stages, giving a fine sense of achievement when the summit
is gained. Catstycam should be avoided in bad weather.

THE SUMMIT

Sheffield Pike   Place Fell   Birkhouse Moor

Catstycam is a true peak, and its small shapely summit is the finest in the eastern fells; if it were rock and not mainly grass it would be the finest in the district. Here the highest point is not in doubt!

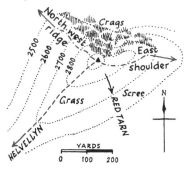

North-west Ridge
2500
2600
2700
2800
Crags
East shoulder
Grass
Scree
RED TARN
N
HELVELLYN
YARDS
0   100   200

DESCENTS: The quickest and easiest descent is by the east shoulder to Glenridding. The north-west ridge is easy but too steep for comfort. For Patterdale, incline right from the east shoulder and cross Red Tarn Beck high up, to join the Striding Edge path.

In bad conditions use the east shoulder, keeping right rather than left in mist, to Red Tarn Beck and so down to Glenridding.

KEPPELCOVE TARN
AND ITS ENVIRONS
— a study in devastation

The burst banks

The breached dam

Keppelcove Tarn is now a marsh. Formerly it served as a reservoir for the Glenridding lead mine. In October 1927, following a cloudburst, flooded waters burst the banks of the tarn, carved out a new ravine, and caused great damage. The dam was breached later, in 1931, and has never been repaired.

The North-west Ridge, from White Side

THE VIEW

Catstycam, like all the satellites of Helvellyn,
is robbed of a comprehensive view by
Helvellyn itself, close at hand and
higher. There is, however, an array
of distant fells over the saddle
between Helvellyn Lower Man
and White Side. Eastwards
the prospect is good.

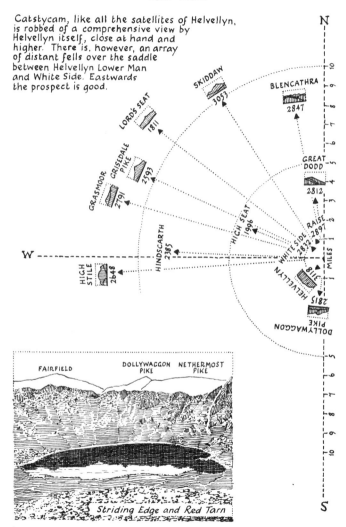

Striding Edge and Red Tarn

THE VIEW

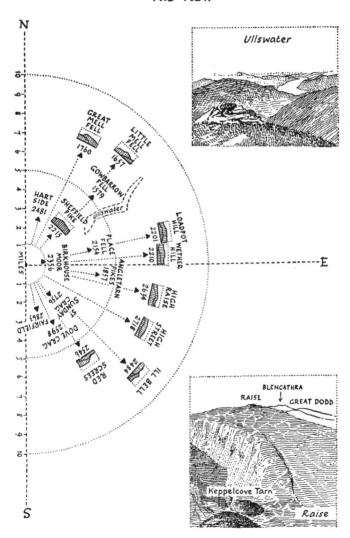

Clough Head 2381'

from High Rigg

● Threlkeld

Wanthwaite
●
▲ CLOUGH
HEAD

▲ GREAT
DODD

● Legburthwaite

MILES

0   1   2   3

From Kirkstone Pass the massive main
ridge of the Fairfield and Helvellyn fells
runs north, mile after mile, throughout
maintaining a consistently high and a
remarkably uniform altitude, and with
a dozen distinct summits over 2500! At
its northern extremity the ground falls
away swiftly to the deep valley of the
Glenderamackin, and the last outpost
of the ridge, although not so elevated
as the summits to the south, occupies a
commanding site : this is Clough Head.

NATURAL FEATURES

Contrary to the usual pattern of the Helvellyn fells, of which it is the most northerly member, Clough Head displays its crags to the west and grassy slopes to the east. These crags form a steep, continuous, mile-long wall above St John's-in-the-Vale, with one breach only where a walker may safely venture; they are riven by deep gullies, one of which (Sandbed Gill) is the rockiest and roughest watercourse in the Helvellyn range. After initial steep scree, the northern slopes descend gently to the wide valley of the Glenderamackin at Threlkeld. Clough Head is an interesting fell, not only for walkers and explorers but for the ornithologist and botanist, the geologist and antiquarian also; while the merely curious traveller may content himself by puzzling out why and for what purpose Fisher's wife trod so persistently that remarkable path to Jim's Fold.

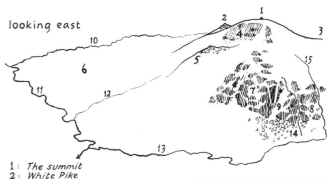

looking east

1 : The summit
2 : White Pike
3 : Ridge continuing to Great Dodd
4 : Red Screes
5 : Threlkeld Knotts
6 : Threlkeld Common
7 : Wanthwaite Crags
8 : Bram Crag
9 : Fisher's Wife's Rake
10 : Mosedale Beck
11 : River Glenderamackin
12 : Birkett Beck
13 : St John's Beck
14 : Sandbed Gill
15 : Beckthorns Gill

Wanthwaite Crags

MAP

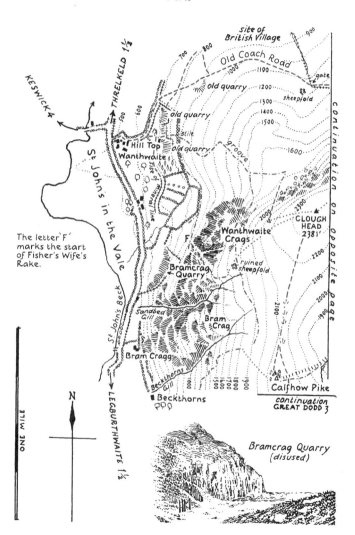

site of British Village

Old Coach Road

900

700 800

1000 1100

gate

old quarry 1200

sheepfold

1300

1400

1500

old quarry

600

stile

Hill Top

Wanthwaite

old quarry

groove

1600

THRELKELD 1½

KESWICK 4

St John's in the Vale

500

Mineral Line

2000

CLOUGH
HEAD
2381

2100

2200

The letter 'F'
marks the start
of Fisher's Wife's
Rake.

F

Wanthwaite
Crags

ruined
sheepfold

Bramcrag
Quarry

2100

Sandbed
Gill

Bram
Crag

2000

1900

St John's Beck

Bram Cragg

2000

1800

1700

1600

1500

Beckthorns
Gill

Beckthorns

Calfhow Pike

continuation
GREAT DODD 3

ONE MILE

N

LEGBURTHWAITE 1½

continuation on opposite page

Bramcrag Quarry
(disused)

MAP

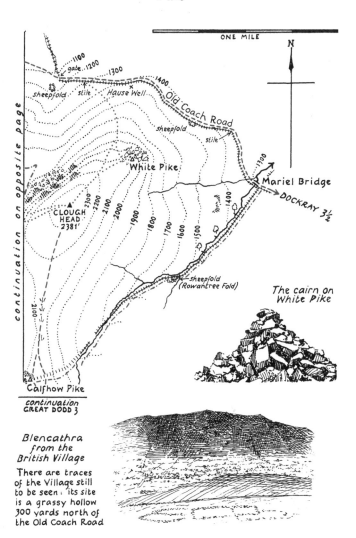

ONE MILE

N

1100
gate..1200
1300
1400
Old Coach Road
sheepfold   stile   Hause Well   ×
sheepfold
stile
White Pike
1700
Mariel Bridge
DOCKRAY 3½
2300
2200
2100
2000
1900
1800
1700
1600
1500
1400
▲ CLOUGH
HEAD
2381'
continuation on opposite page
2100
sheepfold
(Rowantree Fold)

The cairn on
White Pike

Calfhow Pike

continuation
GREAT DODD 3

*Blencathra
from the
British Village*

There are traces
of the Village still
to be seen : its
site is a grassy hollow
300 yards north of
the Old Coach Road

ASCENT FROM WANTHWAITE
1900 feet of ascent ; 2 miles ; 3 by way of White Pike

'Wanthwaite' is pronounced 'Wanthet'
and 'Lowthwaite' 'Lowthet'

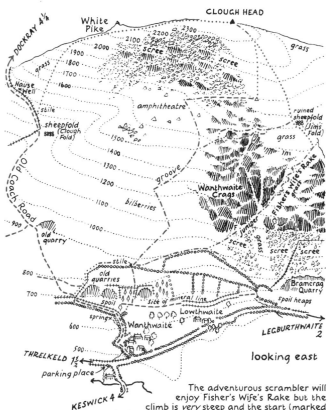

looking east

The adventurous scrambler will
enjoy Fisher's Wife's Rake but the
climb is *very* steep and the start (marked
by 'F' on the diagram here) is difficult to find: turn
left after passing a rowan tree. A much easier route is by the grass
slope up towards White Pike. The intermediate route ends with a choice
of paths, one a 'sporting' high-level crossing of the crags to Jim's Fold.

THE SUMMIT

The top of the fell is a pleasant grassy sward, adorned with a small wall-shelter and an Ordnance Survey column.

Skiddaw

DESCENTS: Fisher's Wife's Rake is difficult to locate from above and in any case is too steep to provide a comfortable way down. The high-level path from Jim's Fold is an interesting route to the easier ground below the crags. Easiest of all is the grass slope to the Old Coach Road below Hause Well.

In bad weather conditions Clough Head is a dangerous place. All steep ground should be avoided and the descent made down the easy grass slope north-north-east to the Old Coach Road. A descent by Fisher's Wife's Rake should not be contemplated and the natural funnel of Sandbed Gill should be strictly left alone.

Two oddities on Clough Head

Unlike most Lakeland springs, which rise from grass, HAUSE WELL issues from a crevice in rocks. It is not easy to locate – its situation is near the fence bounding the Old Coach Road.

SANDBED GILL, a considerable stream in its rocky gorge, has an empty bed at valley-level.

RIDGE ROUTE

To GREAT DODD, 2812': 2 miles
SSW then SE and E
Depression at 2100'
720 feet of ascent
An easy walk on grass

This walk would be completely devoid of interest but for an odd outcrop midway, a welcome oasis of rock in a desert of grass — this is Calfhow Pike. Beyond, the long uphill trudge seems longer than it is, and longer still on a hot day.

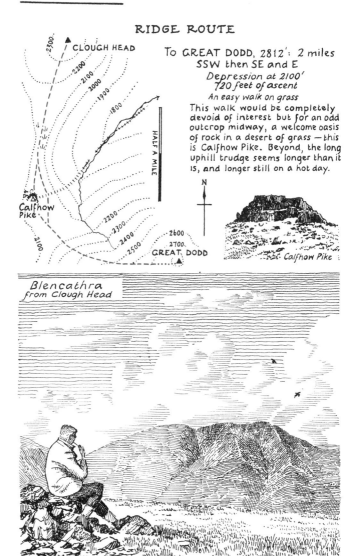

CLOUGH HEAD

2300
2200
2100
2000
1900
1800

HALF A MILE

Calfhow Pike

2200
2300
2400
2500
2600
2700
GREAT DODD

N

Calfhow Pike

Blencathra
from Clough Head

THE VIEW

Clough Head is sufficiently isolated to afford an uninterrupted prospect in every direction except south-east. A special feature, rare in views from the heights of the Helvellyn range, is the nice combination of valley and mountain scenery. This is an excellent viewpoint, the skyline between south and west being especially striking.

Principal Fells

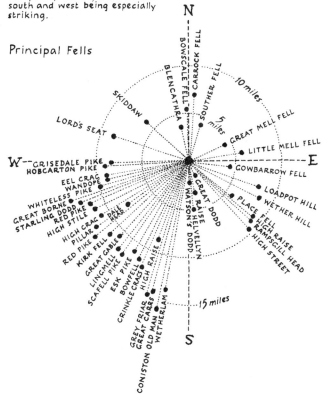

Lakes and Tarns
SW: *Thirlmere*
W: *Derwent Water*
WNW: *Tewet Tarn*
WNW: *Bassenthwaite Lake*

Dollywaggon Pike 2815'

from Deepdale Hause

Patterdale
▲ HELVELLYN
Wythburn
DOLLYWAGGON PIKE
▲ FAIRFIELD

Grasmere
MILES
0   1   2   3   4   5

NATURAL FEATURES

Like most of the high fells south of the Sticks Pass, Dollywaggon Pike exhibits a marked contrast in its western and eastern aspects. To the west, uninteresting grass slopes descend to Dunmail Raise almost unrelieved by rock and scarred only by the wide stony track gouged across the breast of the fell by the boots of generations of pilgrims to Helvellyn. But the eastern side is a desolation of crag and boulder and scree: here are silent recesses rarely visited by walkers but well worth a detailed exploration.

looking north-west

1 The summit of
   Dollywaggon Pike
2 Ridge continuing to
   Nethermost Pike
3 The Tongue
4 Ruthwaite Cove
5 Cock Cove
6 Falcon Crag (or
   Dollywaggon Crag)
7 The three gullies
   of Tarn Crag
8 Tarn Crag
9 Spout Crag
10 Caves (artificial)
11 Birkside Gill
12 Raise Beck
13 Ruthwaite Beck
14 Grisedale Beck
15 Grisedale Tarn

Falcon Crag

The figure 10 also indicates the position of RUTHWAITE LODGE
(built in 1854 as a shooting lodge, but now a climbers' hut)

MAP

A path follows the intake wall to
the north from Dunmail Raise and
crosses two branches of Birkside
Gill by wooden footbridges. There
is a good view of a waterfall from
one bridge, and a water-slide
is overlooked by the other.

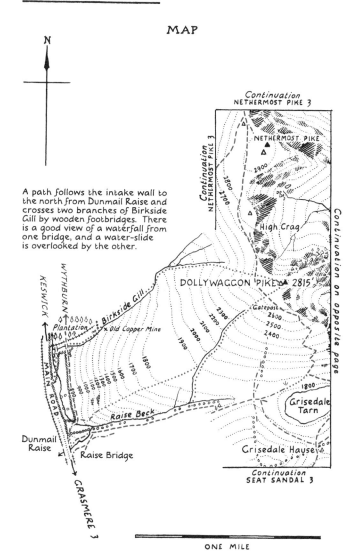

ONE MILE

MAP

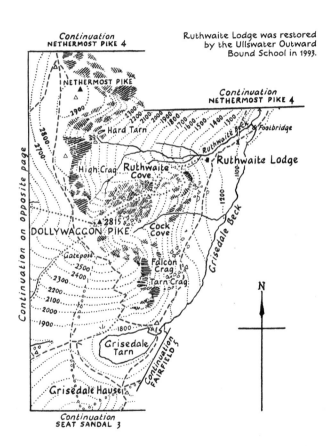

Ruthwaite Lodge was restored
by the Ullswater Outward
Bound School in 1993.

ONE MILE

ASCENT FROM GRASMERE
2700 feet of ascent : 5 miles from Grasmere Church

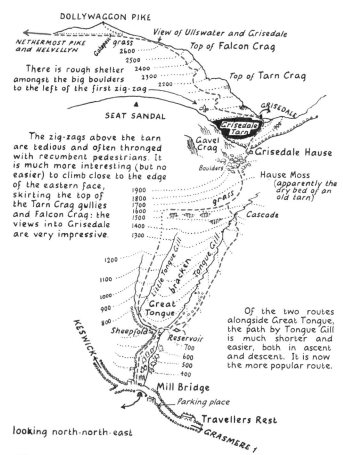

DOLLYWAGGON PIKE

← NETHERMOST PIKE and HELVELLYN

grass
2600
2500
2400
2300
2200

View of Ullswater and Grisedale
Top of Falcon Crag

Top of Tarn Crag

There is rough shelter amongst the big boulders to the left of the first zig-zag

▲ SEAT SANDAL

GRISEDALE

Grisedale Tarn

Gavel Crag

Grisedale Hause

Boulders

The zig-zags above the tarn are tedious and often thronged with recumbent pedestrians. It is much more interesting (but no easier) to climb close to the edge of the eastern face, skirting the top of the Tarn Crag gullies and Falcon Crag: the views into Grisedale are very impressive.

Hause Moss (apparently the dry bed of an old tarn)

1900
1800
1700
1600
1500
1400
1300

grass

Cascade

1200
1100
1000
900
800

Little Tongue Gill

bracken

Tongue Gill

Great Tongue

KESWICK →

Sheepfold

Reservoir

700
600
500
400

Of the two routes alongside Great Tongue, the path by Tongue Gill is much shorter and easier, both in ascent and descent. It is now the more popular route.

Mill Bridge

Parking place

Travellers Rest

GRASMERE 1

looking north-north-east

The route illustrated is the much-trodden path, almost a highway in places, from Grasmere to Helvellyn. It climbs the breast of Dollywaggon Pike and passes slightly below its summit, which is easily attained by a short detour.

ASCENT FROM DUNMAIL RAISE
2100 feet of ascent : 2 miles

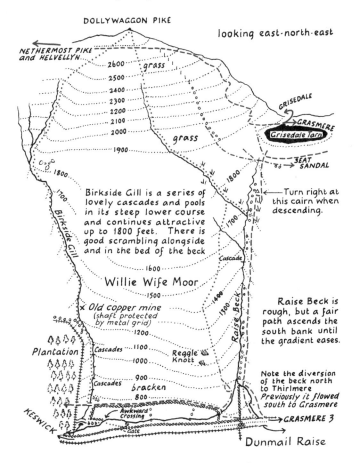

DOLLYWAGGON PIKE

looking east-north-east

← NETHERMOST PIKE and HELVELLYN

2600
2500
2400
2300
2200
2100
2000

grass

1900

grass

GRISEDALE

GRASMERE

Grisedale Tarn

SEAT SANDAL

1800

← Turn right at this cairn when descending.

1700

Cascade

Birkside Gill is a series of lovely cascades and pools in its steep lower course and continues attractive up to 1800 feet. There is good scrambling alongside and in the bed of the beck

Birkside Gill

1600

Willie Wife Moor

1500

1400

Raise Beck is rough, but a fair path ascends the south bank until the gradient eases.

× Old copper mine (shaft protected by metal grid)

1300

Raise Beck

1200

Plantation

Cascades   1100

1000

Reggle Knott

Note the diversion of the beck north to Thirlmere. Previously it flowed south to Grasmere

Cascades   900

bracken

800

KESWICK

Awkward Crossing

→ GRASMERE 3

Gate

Dunmail Raise

The western slopes offer a short and direct route from the main road but are monotonously grassy and of greater interest to sheep than to walkers. Preferably one of the two becks should be followed up, especially on a hot day.

ASCENT FROM GRISEDALE
2400 feet of ascent · 5 miles from Patterdale village

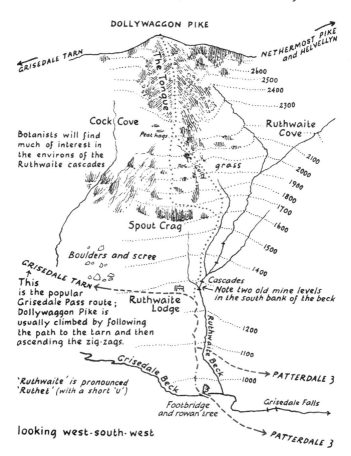

DOLLYWAGGON PIKE

GRISEDALE TARN

NETHERMOST PIKE and HELVELLYN

The Tongue

Cock Cove

Peat hags

Botanists will find much of interest in the environs of the Ruthwaite cascades

Ruthwaite Cove

grass

2600
2500
2400
2300
2100
2000
1900
1800
1700
1600
1500
1400

Spout Crag

Boulders and scree

GRISEDALE TARN

This is the popular Grisedale Pass route; Dollywaggon Pike is usually climbed by following the path to the tarn and then ascending the zig-zags.

Cascades
Note two old mine levels in the south bank of the beck

Ruthwaite Lodge

Ruthwaite Beck

1200

1100

1000

PATTERDALE 3

'Ruthwaite' is pronounced 'Ruthet' (with a short 'u')

Grisedale Beck

Footbridge and rowan tree

Grisedale Falls

PATTERDALE 3

looking west·south·west

This is much the most interesting and exhilarating way to the summit, but it is relatively unknown and rarely used. The finish up the narrow Tongue is excellent. *This route should not be attempted in bad weather conditions.*

THE SUMMIT

The summit is a small grassy dome, narrowing to the east. The big cairn is 30 yards west of the highest point. The fence post has gone.

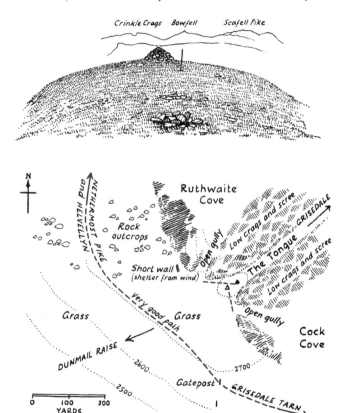

DESCENTS: The quickest and easiest way off is the direct descent to Dunmail Raise, but Birkside Gill should be avoided. The Tongue route should not be attempted, nor descents made into Cock Cove or Ruthwaite Cove, *in mist*: this side of the fell is extremely rough. |||| *In bad weather conditions*, the safest descent is to Grisedale Tarn by the zig-zag path, for either Grasmere or Patterdale.

THE VIEW

The view is extensive in most directions but restricted in the north and south-east by neighbouring fells of greater altitude. Westwards, the panorama is excellent.

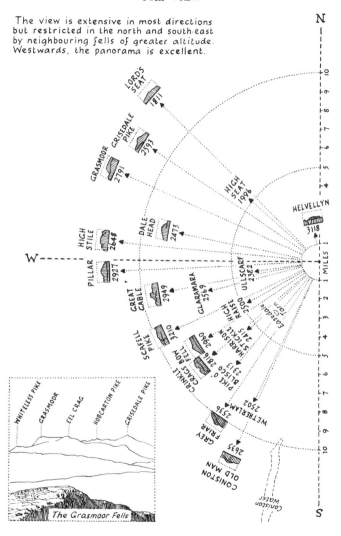

N

W

MILES

S

LORDS SEAT
1811

GRISEDALE PIKE
2593

GRASMOOR
2791

HIGH SEAT
1996

HELVELLYN
3118

DALE HEAD
2473

HIGH STILE
2648

PILLAR
2927

GREAT GABLE
2949

GLARAMARA
2569

ULLSCARF
2382

EASEDALE TARN

HIGH RAISE
2500

SCAFELL PIKE
3210

HARRISON STICKLE
2415

PIKE o' BLISCO
2313

CRINKLE CRAGS
2816

BOW FELL
2960

WETHERLAM
2502

GREY FRIAR
2536

CONISTON OLD MAN
2635

Coniston Water

The Grasmoor Fells

WHITELESS PIKE

GRASMOOR

EEL CRAG

HOBCARTON PIKE

GRISEDALE PIKE

THE VIEW

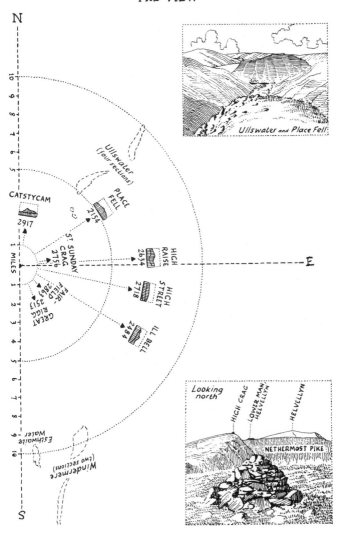

N

10
9
8
7
6
5

Ulfswater
(four sections)

CATSTYCAM

PLACE
FELL
2154

2917

ST SUNDAY
CRAG
2756

HIGH
RAISE
2634

1 MILES

E

FAIR FIELD 2863
RIGG 2513
GREAT

HIGH
STREET
2718

1
2
3

ILL
BELL
2484

4
5
6
7
8
9

Esthwaite Water

10

Windermere
(two sections)

S

Ullswater and Place Fell

Looking north

HIGH CRAG

LOWER MAN
HELVELLYN

HELVELLYN

NETHERMOST PIKE

Cave and Cascades, Ruthwaite

RIDGE ROUTES

To NETHERMOST PIKE, 2920′ : 1 mile : NW then N.

Depression at 2700′
220 feet of ascent

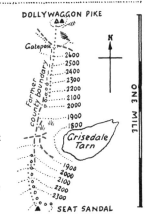

An easy walk with fine views. Safe in mist if the path is followed closely.

An excellent path links Dollywaggon Pike and Nethermost Pike, skirting their actual summits to the west. A more interesting route (no path) lies along the edge of the crags overlooking Ruthwaite Cove.

To SEAT SANDAL, 2415′
1¼ miles : S

Depression at 1850′
600 feet of ascent

A steep but easy descent followed by a dull climb. The depression is marshy. Safe but unpleasant in mist.

Seat Sandal is the next fell to the south, but the direct route to it can hardly be called a ridge. There is no path, but the way is indicated by broken fences and walls.

The Tarn Crag gullies

Dove Crag 2598'

from Dovedale

Patterdale ●

Hartsop ●

▲ FAIRFIELD

DOVE ▲ CRAG

RED SCREES ▲

● Grasmere

Ambleside
●

MILES
0   1   2   3   4

The lofty height that towers so magnificently over Dovedale is indebted for its name to a very impressive vertical wall of rock on its north-east flank: the crag was named first and the summit of the parent fell above, which fifty years ago was considered unworthy of any official title, is now named 'Dove Crag' on the Ordnance Survey maps.

NATURAL FEATURES

Dove Crag is a mountain of sharp contrasts. To the east, its finest aspect, it presents a scarred and rugged face, a face full of character and interest. Here, in small compass, is a tangle of rough country, a maze of steep cliffs, gloomy hollows and curious foothills gnarled like the knuckles of a clenched fist, with the charming valley of Dovedale below and the main crag frowning down over all. Very different is its appearance from other directions. A high ridge runs south, with featureless grass slopes flowing down from it to the valleys of Rydale and Scandale. The fell is a vertebra of the Fairfield spine and is connected to the next height in the system, Hart Crag, by a lofty depression.

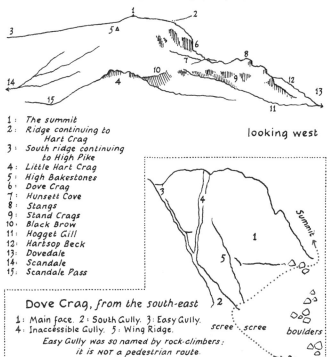

looking west

1: The summit
2: Ridge continuing to Hart Crag
3: South ridge continuing to High Pike
4: Little Hart Crag
5: High Bakestones
6: Dove Crag
7: Hunsett Cove
8: Stangs
9: Stand Crags
10: Black Brow
11: Hogget Gill
12: Hartsop Beck
13: Dovedale
14: Scandale
15: Scandale Pass

Dove Crag, *from the south-east*

1: Main face. 2: South Gully. 3: Easy Gully.
4: Inaccessible Gully. 5: Wing Ridge.
Easy Gully was so named by rock-climbers: it is NOT a pedestrian route.

MAP

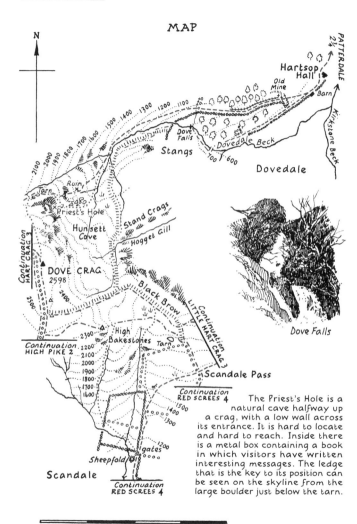

Dove Falls

The Priest's Hole is a natural cave halfway up a crag, with a low wall across its entrance. It is hard to locate and hard to reach. Inside there is a metal box containing a book in which visitors have written interesting messages. The ledge that is the key to its position can be seen on the skyline from the large boulder just below the tarn.

ASCENT FROM PATTERDALE
2,200 feet of ascent: 5 miles from Patterdale village

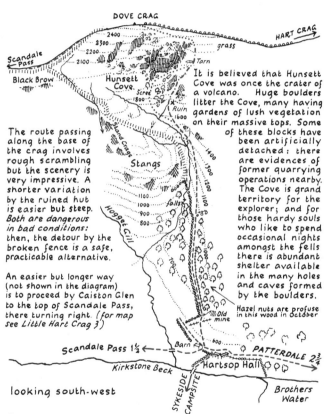

The route passing along the base of the crag involves rough scrambling but the scenery is very impressive. A shorter variation by the ruined hut is easier but steep. *Both are dangerous in bad conditions:* then, the detour by the broken fence is a safe, practicable alternative.

An easier but longer way (not shown in the diagram) is to proceed by Caiston Glen to the top of Scandale Pass, there turning right. (*for map see Little Hart Crag 3*)

It is believed that Hunsett Cove was once the crater of a volcano. Huge boulders litter the Cove, many having gardens of lush vegetation on their massive tops. Some of these blocks have been artificially detached: there are evidences of former quarrying operations nearby. The Cove is grand territory for the explorer; and for those hardy souls who like to spend occasional nights amongst the fells there is abundant shelter available in the many holes and caves formed by the boulders.

Hazel nuts are profuse in this wood in October

looking south-west

Dove Crag is most often ascended from Ambleside on the popular tour of the 'Fairfield Horseshoe' — but the climb from Patterdale, by Dovedale, is far superior: it gives a much more interesting and intimate approach, the sharp transition from the soft loveliness of the valley to the desolation above being very impressive.

ASCENT FROM AMBLESIDE
2500 feet of ascent : 5 miles

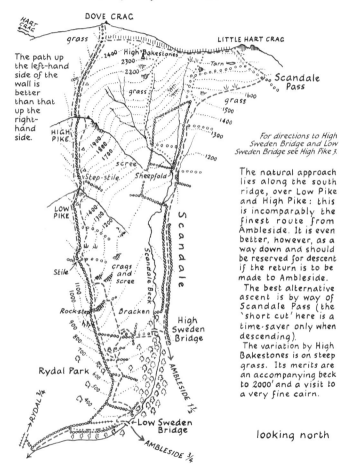

The path up the left-hand side of the wall is better than that up the right-hand side.

For directions to High Sweden Bridge and Low Sweden Bridge see High Pike 3.

The natural approach lies along the south ridge, over Low Pike and High Pike: this is incomparably the finest route from Ambleside. It is even better, however, as a way down and should be reserved for descent if the return is to be made to Ambleside.

The best alternative ascent is by way of Scandale Pass (the 'short cut' here is a time-saver only when descending).

The variation by High Bakestones is on steep grass. Its merits are an accompanying beck to 2000' and a visit to a very fine cairn.

looking north

Dove Crag cannot be seen from Ambleside, but rising from the fields north of the town is its clearly-defined south ridge, offering an obvious staircase to the summit.

THE SUMMIT

The actual top of the fell is a small rock platform crowned by a cairn, twenty yards east of the crumbling wall crossing the broad summit-plateau. It is of little distinction and there is nothing of interest in the immediate surroundings.

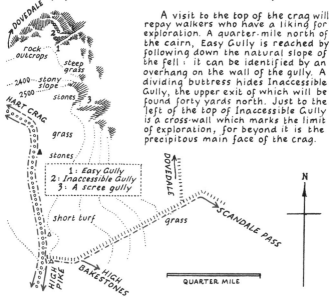

A visit to the top of the crag will repay walkers who have a liking for exploration. A quarter-mile north of the cairn, Easy Gully is reached by following down the natural slope of the fell: it can be identified by an overhang on the wall of the gully. A dividing buttress hides Inaccessible Gully, the upper exit of which will be found forty yards north. Just to the left of the top of Inaccessible Gully is a cross-wall which marks the limit of exploration, for beyond it is the precipitous main face of the crag.

1: Easy Gully
2: Inaccessible Gully
3: A scree gully

DESCENTS: All routes of ascent may be reversed for descent but the way down into Dovedale by the base of the crag is very rough. The High Bakestones route to Scandale is not recommended. *In mist, whether bound for Ambleside or Patterdale, follow the broken wall south, soon turning left along the broken fence for Patterdale via Dovedale or Scandale Pass. Direct descents to Dovedale from the summit must not be attempted.*

THE VIEW

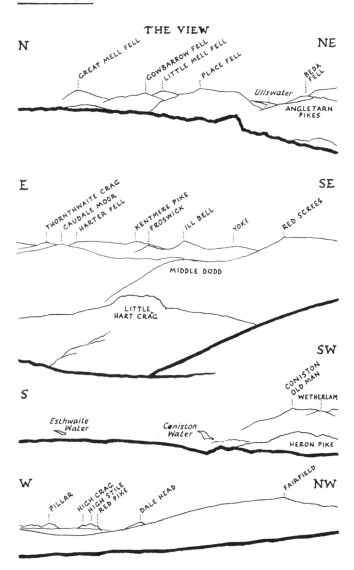

THE VIEW

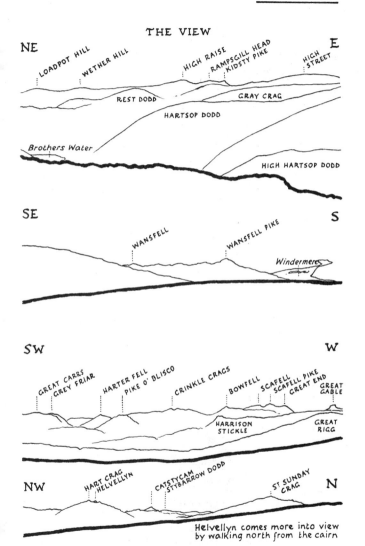

NE / E

LOADPOT HILL
WETHER HILL
HIGH RAISE
RAMPSGILL HEAD
KIDSTY PIKE
HIGH STREET
REST DODD
GRAY CRAG
HARTSOP DODD
Brothers Water
HIGH HARTSOP DODD

SE / S

WANSFELL
WANSFELL PIKE
Windermere

SW / W

GREAT CARRS
GREY FRIAR
HARTER FELL
PIKE O' BLISCO
CRINKLE CRAGS
BOWFELL
SCAFELL
SCAFELL PIKE
GREAT END
GREAT GABLE
HARRISON STICKLE
GREAT RIGG

NW / N

HART CRAG
HELVELLYN
CATSTYCAM
STYBARROW DODD
ST SUNDAY CRAG

Helvellyn comes more into view
by walking north from the cairn

RIDGE ROUTES

To HART CRAG, 2698': ¾ mile : NW

Depression at 2350'
350 feet of ascent

An easy walk but Hart Crag
is not safe in mist.

Follow the broken wall, hardly a yard of which is still standing, until it comes to an end, then clamber up the rocks to the eastern cairn on top of Hart Crag.

To HIGH PIKE, 2155': 1 mile : S

Slight depression
Only a few feet of ascent

One of the easiest miles in Lakeland; grass all the way. Perfectly safe in mist.

Follow the wall south; an intermittent path keeps a few yards to the left of it.

To LITTLE HART CRAG

2091' : 1¼ miles
S then ENE and SE

Minor depressions
200 feet of ascent

Rough grass; may be marshy in places. Little Hart Crag is dangerous in bad conditions.

Follow first the wall south and then the broken fence: it reaches within 200 yards of the summit before turning down towards Scandale Pass.

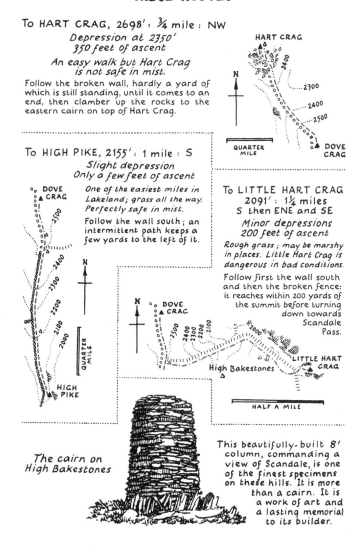

The cairn on High Bakestones

This beautifully-built 8' column, commanding a view of Scandale, is one of the finest specimens on these hills. It is more than a cairn. It is a work of art and a lasting memorial to its builder.

Dovedale, from the top of Easy Gully

Fairfield

2863'

HELVELLYN
▲

Patterdale ●

▲ ST SUNDAY CRAG

▲ FAIRFIELD

▲ DOVE CRAG

● Grasmere

● Rydal

● Ambleside

MILES

0 1 2 3 4

from Grisedale Tarn

NATURAL FEATURES

The rough triangle formed by Grisedale Pass, the Rothay valley and Scandale Pass, with the village of Patterdale as its apex, contains within its area a bulky mountain-system with five distinct summits over 2500'. High ridges link these summits; there are also subsidiary ridges and spurs of lesser altitude, massive rocky buttresses, gloomy coves and fine daleheads. The whole mass constitutes a single geographical unit and the main summit is Fairfield, a grand mountain with grand satellites in support. No group of fells in the district exhibits a more striking contrast in appearance when surveyed from opposite sides than this lofty Fairfield group. From the south it appears as a great horseshoe of grassy slopes below a consistently high skyline, simple in design and impressive in altitude, but lacking those dramatic qualities that appeal most to the lover of hills. But on the north side the Fairfield range is magnificent: here are dark precipices, long fans of scree, abrupt crags, desolate combes and deep valleys: a tangle of rough country, small in extent but full of interest, and well worth exploration. This grimmer side of the Fairfield group can only be visited conveniently from the Patterdale area. Fairfield turns its broad back to the south, to Rydal and Grasmere, and climbers from this direction get only the merest glimpse of its best features; many visitors to the summit, indeed, return unsuspecting, and remember Fairfield and its neighbours as mountains of grass. The few who know the head of Deepdale and the recesses of Dovedale, intimately, have a very different impression.

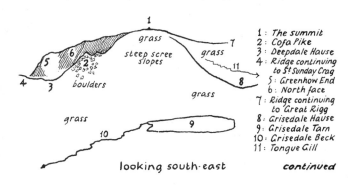

1 : The summit
2 : Cofa Pike
3 : Deepdale Hause
4 : Ridge continuing to St Sunday Crag
5 : Greenhow End
6 : North face
7 : Ridge continuing to Great Rigg
8 : Grisedale Hause
9 : Grisedale Tarn
10 : Grisedale Beck
11 : Tongue Gill

looking south-east

continued

NATURAL FEATURES
continued

Three ridges leave the top of Fairfield: one goes south over Great Rigg to end abruptly at Nab Scar above Rydal Water; another, the spine of the Fairfield system, keeps a high level to Dove Crag, traversing Hart Crag on the way, and the third, and best, runs north inclining east over the splintered crest of Cofa Pike and on to St Sunday Crag. On the west flank only is there no descending ridge: here an ill-defined gable-end falls steeply to Grisedale Hause.

The southern and western slopes are simple, the northern and eastern complicated and far more interesting. Here a mile-long face of alternating rock and scree towers high above the barren hollow of Deepdale. Crags abound: most impressive is the precipitous cliff of Greenhow End, scarped on three sides and thrusting far into the valley, and a wall of even steeper rock, with Scrubby Crag prominent, bounds Link Cove to the east.

Fairfield claims Deepdale Beck, Rydal Beck and the main branch of Tongue Gill as its streams, but is only one of many contributors to Grisedale Beck. It is without a tarn of its own, forming one side only of the green basin containing Grisedale Tarn.

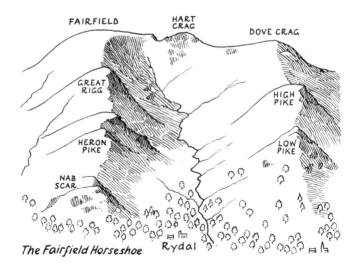

The Fairfield Horseshoe

Cofa Pike and the north-east ridge

Greenhow End

Scrubby Crag

The Crags
of
Fairfield

Black Crag, Rydal Head

MAP

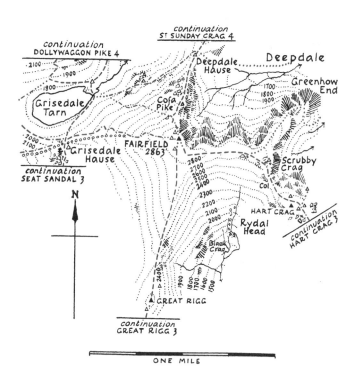

continuation
ST SUNDAY CRAG 4

continuation
DOLLYWAGGON PIKE 4

Deepdale
Hause

Deepdale

Greenhow
End

·2100·
·1900·
1800

1700
1800
1900

Grisedale
Tarn

Cofa
Pike

·2000·
·2100·

Grisedale
Hause

FAIRFIELD
2863

Scrubby
Crag

2800
2700
2600
2500
2400

2300

continuation
SEAT SANDAL 3

Col

2200

2100
2000

HART CRAG

continuation
HART CRAG 3

N

Rydal
Head

Black
Crag

2400

1900
1800
1700
1600
1500

GREAT RIGG

continuation
GREAT RIGG 3

ONE MILE

Rocks on Cofa Pike

ASCENT FROM GRASMERE
2650 feet of ascent : 4¼ miles from Grasmere Church

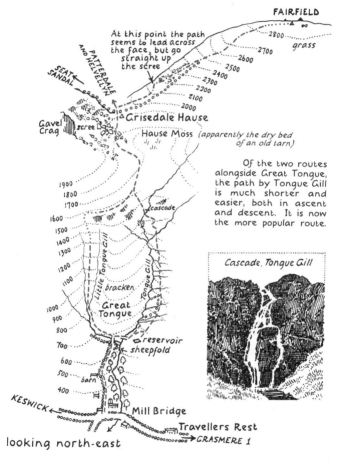

FAIRFIELD

2800

grass

2700

2600

2500

2400

2300

2200

2100

2000

At this point the path seems to lead across the face, but go straight up the scree

SEAT SANDAL

PATTERDALE AND HELVELLYN

Grisedale Hause

Gavel Crag

scree

Hause Moss *(apparently the dry bed of an old tarn)*

Of the two routes alongside Great Tongue, the path by Tongue Gill is much shorter and easier, both in ascent and descent. It is now the more popular route.

1900
1800
1700
1600
1500
1400
1300
1200
1100
1000
900
800
700
600
500
400

cascade

Little Tongue Gill

Tongue Gill

bracken

Great Tongue

reservoir
sheepfold

barn

Cascade, Tongue Gill

KESWICK ←

Mill Bridge

Travellers Rest
→ GRASMERE 1

looking north-east

The path to Grisedale Hause, keeping right of the Tongue, is distinct but above the Hause there is scree to negotiate. Tongue Gill is an interesting approach but the last 1000' of climbing is dull. The top of Fairfield is confusing in mist.

ASCENT FROM PATTERDALE
2400 feet of ascent : 5½ miles

looking south-west

This is a most impressive approach. The towering cliffs of Greenhow End and the mile-long facade of imposing crags and deep-riven gullies on Fairfield's north-east face are ample recompense for the immediate dreariness of Deepdale.

If the return is to be made to Patterdale over St Sunday Crag (as it should be if the weather is good) the route would have to be retraced as far as Deepdale Hause. This is no disadvantage over such interesting territory, but walkers who object to going over the same ground twice could use the better-known approach along Grisedale to the wall on Grisedale Hause — beyond the tarn — proceeding thence to the top by the Grasmere route; this alternative is easier. The route over Greenhow End, shown on the diagram, is for experienced scramblers only, in fine weather.

The gradual revelation of the savage northern face of Fairfield as the view up Deepdale unfolds gives a high quality to this route. Deepdale itself is desolate, but has interesting evidences of glacial action; Link Cove is one of the finest examples of a hanging valley.

The head of Deepdale

The cliffs of Fairfield, from Greenhow End

THE SUMMIT

The summit of Fairfield is an extensive grassy plateau. The absence of distinguishing natural features makes it, in mist, particularly confusing, and the abundance of cairns is then a hindrance rather than a help. The actual top is flat and its surface is too rough to bear the imprint of paths, and the one definable point is a tumbledown windbreak of stones, built as a short wall and offering shelter only to persons of imagination. Thirty yards in front of the shelter is the principal and largest cairn, which has five alcoves scooped out of it.

Mention should be made of the excellent turf on this wide top: weary feet will judge it delightful.

DESCENTS : Too many cairns are worse than too few, and it is fortunate that the piles of stones that once adorned the tops of the buttresses of the north face, snares in the mist to strangers to the fell, have now been removed. In clear weather there is no difficulty in identifying the various routes of descent, the best of which lies over Cofa Pike and St Sunday Crag to Patterdale: an exhilarating and beautiful walk.

In mist, note that none of the usual routes descend over steep ground and that a cairn does not necessarily indicate a path. With care, all routes are quite practicable, but the safest way off, in bad weather and whatever the destination, is westwards to Grisedale Tarn, following a line of cairns until a path appears. (It doesn't matter much about finding a path if the walker is sure he is going either west or south, or between these points, but he who wanders northward courts disaster.)

THE SUMMIT

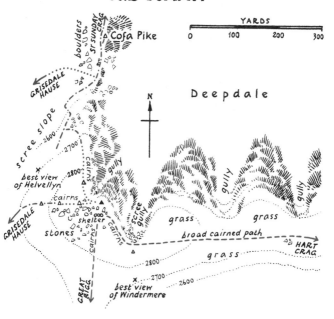

Travellers along the path to Hart Crag are urged to leave it, *in clear weather,* and skirt the edge of the cliffs just to the north, the peeps of Deepdale down the gullies being very impressive. A detour to the top of Greenhow End, easily reached by a gradual descent over grass, is highly recommended, the rock-scenery being especially good and the arête attractive. *This place is dangerous in mist.*

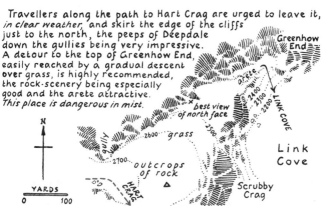

THE VIEW

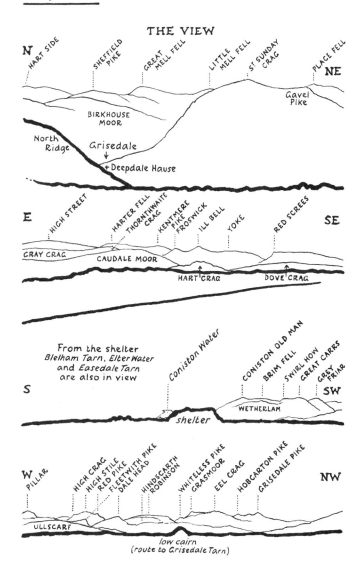

THE VIEW

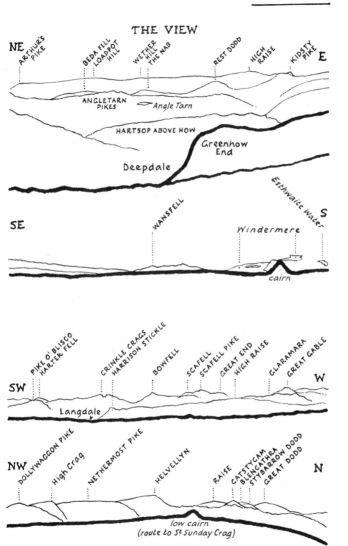

NE

ARTHUR'S PIKE

BEDA FELL
LOADPOT HILL

WETHER HILL
THE NAB

REST DODD

HIGH RAISE

KIDSTY PIKE

E

ANGLETARN PIKES

Angle Tarn

HARTSOP ABOVE HOW

Deepdale

Greenhow End

SE

WANSFELL

Windermere

Esthwaite Water

S

cairn

SW

PIKE O' BLISCO
HARTER FELL

CRINKLE CRAGS
HARRISON STICKLE

BOWFELL

SCAFELL
SCAFELL PIKE

GREAT END
HIGH RAISE

CLARAMARA

GREAT GABLE

W

Langdale

NW

DOLLYWAGGON PIKE

High Crag

NETHERMOST PIKE

HELVELLYN

RAISE

CATSTYCAM
BLENCATHRA
STYBARROW DODD
GREAT DODD

N

low cairn
(route to St Sunday Crag)

RIDGE ROUTES

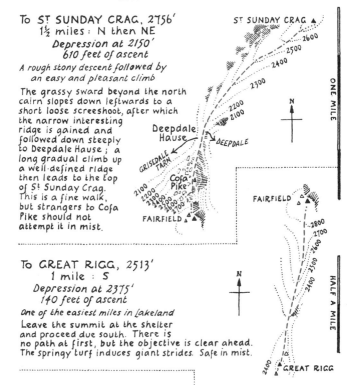

To ST SUNDAY CRAG, 2756'
1½ miles : N then NE
Depression at 2150'
610 feet of ascent
*A rough stony descent followed by
an easy and pleasant climb*

The grassy sward beyond the north
cairn slopes down leftwards to a
short loose screeshoot, after which
the narrow interesting
ridge is gained and
followed down steeply
to Deepdale Hause; a
long gradual climb up
a well-defined ridge
then leads to the top
of St Sunday Crag.
This is a fine walk,
but strangers to Cofa
Pike should not
attempt it in mist.

(map labels) ST SUNDAY CRAG ▲ 2600 2500 2400 2300 2200 2100 ONE MILE N
Deepdale Hause DEEPDALE GRISEDALE TARN Cofa Pike 2200 2300 2400 2500 2600 2700 FAIRFIELD ▲
FAIRFIELD ▲ 2800 2700 2600 2500 2400 2300 2200 2100 HALF A MILE

To GREAT RIGG, 2513'
1 mile : S
Depression at 2375'
140 feet of ascent
One of the easiest miles in Lakeland
Leave the summit at the shelter
and proceed due south. There is
no path at first, but the objective is clear ahead.
The springy turf induces giant strides. Safe in mist.

(map labels) N 2400 ▲ GREAT RIGG

(map labels) FAIRFIELD 2800 2700 2600 2500 2400 N Col HART CRAG ▲ HALF A MILE

To HART CRAG, 2698'
1 mile : E then SE
Depression at 2550'
150 feet of ascent
An easy, interesting walk.
The path across the broad
top of Fairfield is as wide
as a road; it becomes steep
as the col is approached. It is
important, in mist, not to stray
from the path: danger lurks!

The north face of Fairfield

Glenridding Dodd 1450'

from Ullswater
(Sheffield Pike behind)

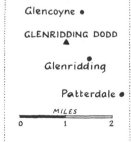

Glencoyne ●

GLENRIDDING DODD ▲

Glenridding ●

Patterdale ●

MILES

0   1   2

Fashions change. When people climbed hills only for the sake of the views, the heathery summit of Glenridding Dodd must have been more frequented than it is today, for once-popular paths of ascent are now overgrown and neglected. It occupies a grand position overlooking the upper reach of Ullswater. It is the end, topographically, of the eastern shoulder of Stybarrow Dodd.

MAP

HALF A MILE

ASCENT FROM GLENRIDDING
1000 feet of ascent

The Dodd is so conveniently situated and offers so delightful a view that it might be expected that walkers would have blazed a wide path to the top. Such is not the case, however, and it is not at all easy to find a way up. The most straightforward route climbs steeply to the left (west) of Blaes Crag (see diagram, Sheffield Pike 4). After crossing the cattle grid bear right. The path passes between an electricity pole and its straining wire and along the foot of an area of scree. A more enjoyable route (avoiding habitation) leaves from the layby to the north of Stybarrow Crag and follows the south side of Mossdale Beck. The woodland is a delight, but there is no continuous path.

THE SUMMIT

On a sunny day in August the summit is a delectable place. Bilberries grow in profusion, and larches almost reach the top on the north side. Many cairns adorn the hummocky summit, the main one overlooking Glenridding village.

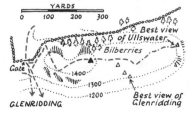

Stybarrow Crag

THE VIEW

Considering the low altitude of the fell, the view is very pleasing: it gains in charm and intimacy what it lacks in extensiveness. Ullswater takes pride of place.

Principal Fells

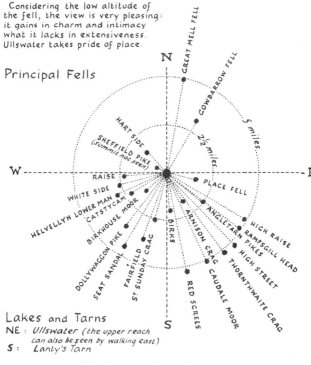

N

GREAT MELL FELL

GOWBARROW FELL

5 miles

2½ miles

HART SIDE

SHEFFIELD PIKE
(summit not seen)

W - E

RAISE

PLACE FELL

WHITE SIDE

HELVELLYN LOWER MAN

CATSTYCAM

HIGH RAISE

BIRKHOUSE MOOR

ANGLETARN PIKES

RAMPSGILL HEAD

HIGH STREET

BIRKS

ARNISON CRAG

HIGH RAISE

DOLLYWAGGON PIKE

SEAT SANDAL

FAIRFIELD

ST SUNDAY CRAG

RED SCREES

CAUDALE MOOR

THORNTHWAITE CRAG

S

Lakes and Tarns

NE : *Ullswater (the upper reach can also be seen by walking east)*

S : *Lanty's Tarn*

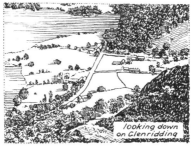

looking down on Glenridding

Ullswater and Birk Fell

Gowbarrow Fell   1579'

from Brown Hills

▲ GREAT MELL FELL

Pooley
Bridge •

LITTLE
MELL ▲
FELL

• Watermillock

▲ GOWBARROW FELL

•
Dockray

• Glenridding

MILES

0   1   2   3   4

NATURAL FEATURES

Gowbarrow Fell is one of the best known of Lakeland's lesser heights, much of it being National Trust property and a favourite playground and picnic-place. It is not the fell itself that brings the crowds, however, and its summit is lonely enough: the great attraction is Aira Force, on the beck forming its western boundary. The fell springs from a mass of high dreary ground in the north and takes the shape of a broad wedge, tapering as it falls to Ullswater, the middle reach of which is its south-eastern boundary throughout. The delightful lower slopes here are beautifully wooded, but low crags and bracken in abundance make them rather difficult of access except where they are traversed by the many pleasant green paths which add so much to Gowbarrow's charms.

The Head of Ullswater
from Green Hill

MAP

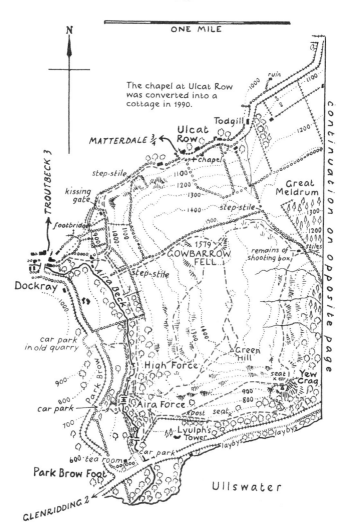

ONE MILE

N

The chapel at Ulcat Row was converted into a cottage in 1990.

MAP

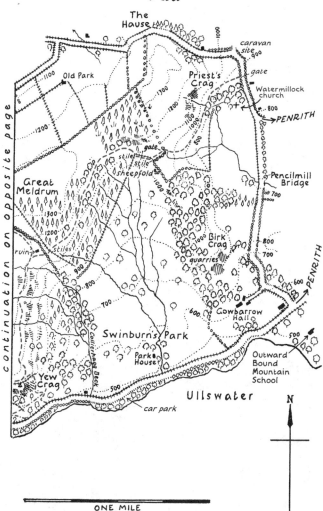

The Hause

caravan site

gate

Priest's Crag

Watermillock church

PENRITH

Old Park

1100

1300

1200

1300

1200

800

gate

stile

stile

sheepfold

Pencilmill Bridge

700

Great Meldrum

1300

1200

1000

Birk Crag

800

700

ruin

stiles

quarries

800

700

900

800

700

600

PENRITH

Gowbarrow Hall

600

Swinburn's Park

500

600

Park House

500

Outward Bound Mountain School

Yew Crag

500

Ullswater

car park

N

continuation on opposite page

ONE MILE

Gowbarrow Fell 5

Aira Force

*Waterfalls,
Aira Beck*

High Force

*Place Fell
and Ullswater
from Gowbarrow Park*

ASCENTS

From Park Brow Foot (the usual starting-place for the climb) a path can be seen rising across the fellside behind Lyulph's Tower to the cairn above Yew Crag: this is the best way to the summit. The path, always interesting, continues to what remains of the shooting box. At one time lost in the marshes, the path can now be followed all the way to the summit. (The shooting box may be reached also by a pleasant path that starts behind Watermillock church and passes through the new plantations. A shorter route from Park Brow Foot goes up the shoulder above Aira Force. The ascent from Dockray direct (by following up the wall) is much less attractive.

Cairn above Yew Crag   *Yew Crag*   *The shooting box (now ruins)*

THE SUMMIT

Great Mell Fell

Flowers, heather and bilberries bloom on the pleasant little ridge where the summit-cairn depicted here once stood, but the neighbourhood is drab. This ridge is fringed on the side facing Ullswater by a wall of short broken crags and there are other outcrops nearby.

DESCENTS: The best way off the fell is over the undulating top to Green Hill, descending from there to Aira Force. If the bracken is high, it is worth while to search for the path.

In mist, join the wall north of the summit, turning left for Dockray, right for the old shooting box (for Watermillock or Park Brow Foot).

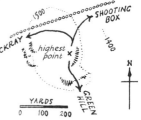

NOTE: In the years since the drawings on this page were prepared, Gowbarrow Fell has lost its summit-cairn but gained an O.S. triangulation column (no. 10790).

The summit-ridge

THE VIEW

Gowbarrow Fell faces up Ullswater into the throat of the deep valley of Patterdale, and a feature of the view is the impressive grouping of the fells steeply enclosing it. Very little of the lake can be seen from the top of the fell because of the intervening high ground. Half a mile south from the summit is a far better viewpoint, Green Hill.

Principal Fells

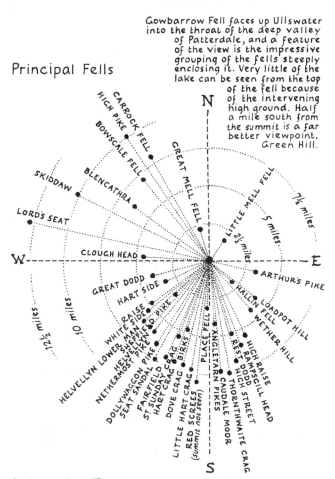

Lakes and Tarns

ENE : Ullswater — the lower reach only. The more attractive upper reaches come into view by walking across the top to Green Hill, where the lake is seen most impressively.

Great Dodd

2812'

Threlkeld

▲ CLOUGH HEAD

Dockray

Fornside

▲ GREAT DODD

Legburthwaite

▲ STYBARROW DODD

▲ RAISE

Glenridding

▲ HELVELLYN

MILES

0 1 2 3 4

from High Rigg

NATURAL FEATURES

Great Dodd, well named, is the most extensive of the fells in the Helvellyn range. To the north-east, its long sprawling slopes fall away gradually in an undulating wilderness of grass to the Old Coach Road; beyond is a wide expanse of uncultivated marshland, not at all characteristic of Lakeland and of no appeal to walkers. North and south, high ground continues the line of the main ridge, but steepening slopes reach valley-level on both east and west flanks. Grass is everywhere: it offers easy and pleasant tramping but no excitements. Rocks are few and far between: there is a broken line of cliffs, Wolf Crags, overlooking the coach road, and the rough breast of High Brow above Dowthwaitehead breaks out in a series of steep crags (a favourite haunt of buzzards), while there are sundry small outcrops on both east and west flanks well below the summit.

Two of Great Dodd's streams are harnessed to provide water supplies: on the west side, Mill Gill, which has a fine ravine, is diverted to Manchester via Thirlmere; on the east, Aira Beck's famous waterfalls are robbed of their full glory to supply the rural districts of Cumbria. Mosedale Beck and Trout Beck drain the dreary wastes to the north.

looking south

1 : The summit
2 : Calfhow Pike
3 : Randerside
4 : High Brow
5 : Stybarrow Dodd
6 : Watson's Dodd
7 : Clough Head
8 : Wolf Crags
9 : Dowthwaite Crag
10 : Lurge Crag
11 : Aira Beck
12 : Trout Beck
13 : Mosedale Beck
14 : Mill Gill
15 : Thirlmere
16 : St John's Beck

MAP

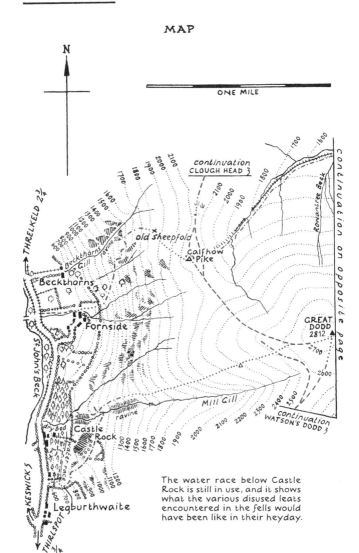

The water race below Castle Rock is still in use, and it shows what the various disused leats encountered in the fells would have been like in their heyday.

MAP

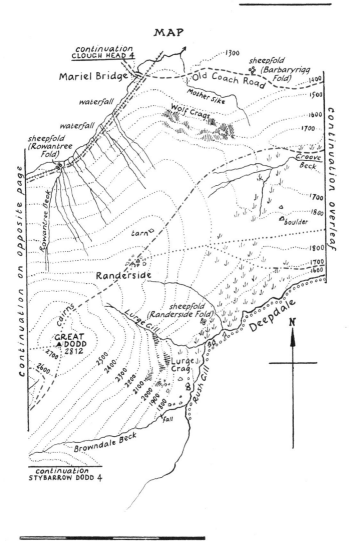

continuation
CLOUGH HEAD 4

Mariel Bridge

1300

sheepfold
(Barbaryrigg
Fold)

Old Coach Road

1400

1500

waterfall

Mother Sike

Wolf Crags

1600

waterfall

1700

sheepfold
(Rowantree
Fold)

continuation overleaf

Groove
Beck

Rowantree Beck

1700

1800

boulder

continuation on opposite page

tarn

1800

1700
1600

Randerside

sheepfold
(Randerside Fold)

88

Deepdale

cairns

Lurge Gill

N

GREAT
DODD
2812

2700

2500

2400

Lurge
Crag

2600

2300

Rush Gill

2200

2100

2000

1900

1800

fall

Browndale Beck

continuation
STYBARROW DODD 4

ONE MILE

MAP

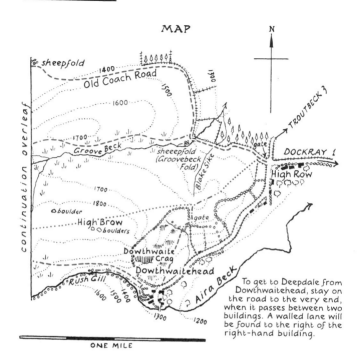

N

sheepfold

1400

Old Coach Road

1500

1600

1600

TROUTBECK 3

1700

Groove Beck

sheepfold
(Groovebeck
Fold)

Blake Sike

gate

DOCKRAY 1

High Row

1700

1800

boulder

High Brow

boulders

gate

Dowthwaite
Crag

Dowthwaitehead

Rush Gill

Aira Beck

1600   1500

1300

1200

To get to Deepdale from
Dowthwaitehead, stay on
the road to the very end,
when it passes between two
buildings. A walled lane will
be found to the right of the
right-hand building.

continuation overleaf

ONE MILE

Wolf Crags

ASCENT FROM DOCKRAY
2000 feet of ascent : 4¼ miles

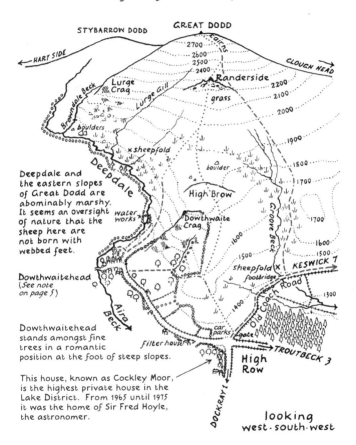

STYBARROW DODD

GREAT DODD

HART SIDE →

2700
2600
2500
2400

cairns

● Randerside

CLOUGH HEAD →

2200
2100
2000
1900

Lurge Crag

Lurge Gill

grass

Braundale Beck

boulders

× sheepfold

□ boulder

1800
1700

Deepdale

Deepdale and the eastern slopes of Great Dodd are abominably marshy. It seems an oversight of nature that the sheep here are not born with webbed feet.

water works

High Brow

Dowthwaite Crag

Groove Beck

1700

1600
1500

1600

1500

Dowthwaitehead
(See note on page 5)

sheepfold ×

KESWICK 7

footbridge

Dowthwaitehead stands amongst fine trees in a romantic position at the foot of steep slopes.

Aira Beck

Old Coach Road

1400

1300

car parks

filter house

gate

High Row

→ TROUTBECK 3

This house, known as Cockley Moor, is the highest private house in the Lake District. From 1965 until 1975 it was the home of Sir Fred Hoyle, the astronomer.

DOCKRAY 1

looking west·south·west

The ascent of Great Dodd *via* Groove Beck is one of the easiest climbs in Lakeland, the gradients being very gentle throughout, but otherwise it is without merit. All routes from Dockray are uninspiring and dreary, and most unpleasant in wet weather.

ASCENT FROM FORNSIDE
2300 feet of ascent : 2½ miles

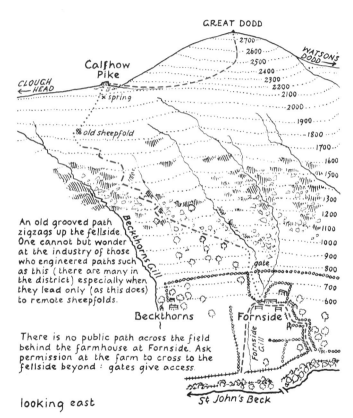

An old grooved path
zigzags up the fellside.
One cannot but wonder
at the industry of those
who engineered paths such
as this (there are many in
the district) especially when
they lead only (as this does)
to remote sheepfolds.

There is no public path across the field
behind the farmhouse at Fornside. Ask
permission at the farm to cross to the
fellside beyond : gates give access.

looking east

  This route is very rarely used. It is steep as far as
the sheepfold, but there is recompense in the lovely
view of the valley above Fornside. Thereafter it is
monotonously grassy, with only the oddity of Calfhow
Pike to relieve the tedium of progress.

ASCENT FROM LEGBURTHWAITE
2300 feet of ascent : 2¼ miles

*Users of Bartholomew's map
should note that Legburthwaite is not indicated thereon*

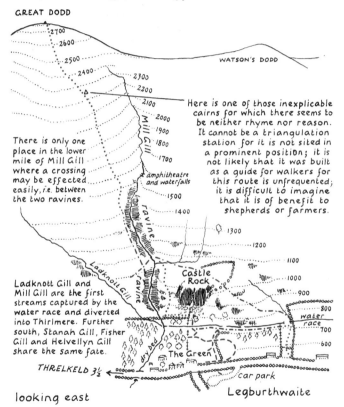

GREAT DODD

2700
2600
2500
2400

WATSON'S DODD

2300
2200
2100
2000
1900
1800
1700

Mill Gill

Here is one of those inexplicable
cairns for which there seems to
be neither rhyme nor reason.
It cannot be a triangulation
station for it is not sited in
a prominent position; it is
not likely that it was built
as a guide for walkers for
this route is unfrequented;
it is difficult to imagine
that it is of benefit to
shepherds or farmers.

There is only one
place in the lower
mile of Mill Gill
where a crossing
may be effected
easily, i.e. between
the two ravines.

amphitheatre
and waterfalls

1500
1400

ravine

1300
1200

Ladknott Gill

ravine

Castle
Rock

1100
1000
900

water
race

800

Ladknott Gill and
Mill Gill are the first
streams captured by the
water race and diverted
into Thirlmere. Further
south, Stanah Gill, Fisher
Gill and Helvellyn Gill
share the same fate.

dry bed

700
600

The Green

THRELKELD 3½

car park

Legburthwaite

looking east

The first part of this route is pleasant enough; it
is interesting also if combined with an exploration
of the environs of Castle Rock, but after crossing
the attractive Mill Gill it develops into a trudge
up a long grass slope : the gradient is easy.

THE SUMMIT

On the north top is the main cairn, and on the south top is another cairn hollowed to provide shelter from the west wind. At one time this was the only cairn, and its builders must have felt twinges of conscience during their task: they selected as its site a most convenient rash of stones, ignoring the highest point a hundred yards distant, where all was grass. The summit is otherwise featureless.

DESCENTS : There are no paths from the summit, but the direction of the route to Dockray is marked by a small cairn which appears on the skyline when viewed from the main cairn.

In mist, direction may be taken from the shelter in the cairn, which faces east.

There is no danger in leaving the top even in the thickest weather, but care must be taken to avoid descending into the inhospitable valley of Deepdale by mistake.

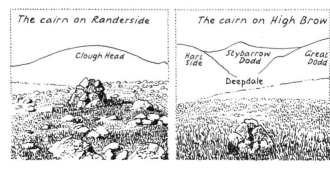

| The cairn on Randerside | The cairn on High Brow |

RIDGE ROUTES

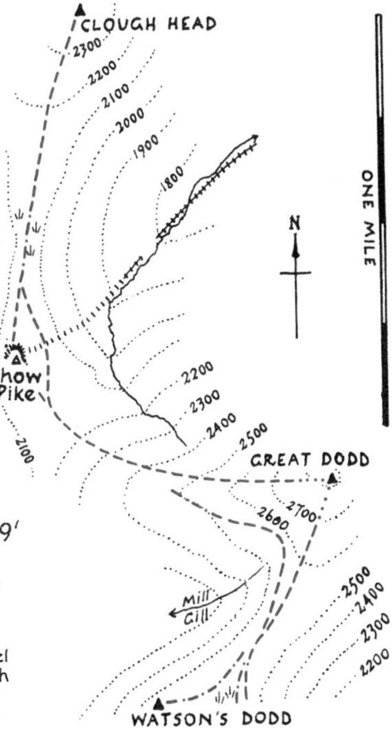

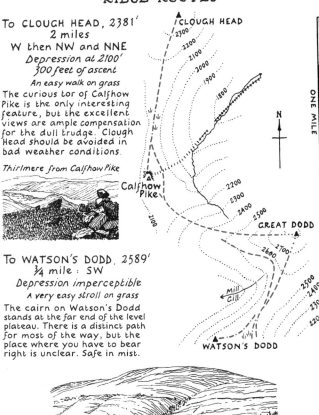

To CLOUGH HEAD, 2381′
2 miles
W then NW and NNE
Depression at 2100′
300 feet of ascent
An easy walk on grass

The curious tor of Calfhow Pike is the only interesting feature, but the excellent views are ample compensation for the dull trudge. Clough Head should be avoided in bad weather conditions.

Thirlmere from Calfhow Pike

To WATSON'S DODD, 2589′
¾ mile : SW
Depression imperceptible
A very easy stroll on grass

The cairn on Watson's Dodd stands at the far end of the level plateau. There is a distinct path for most of the way, but the place where you have to bear right is unclear. Safe in mist.

Dowthwaitehead

THE VIEW

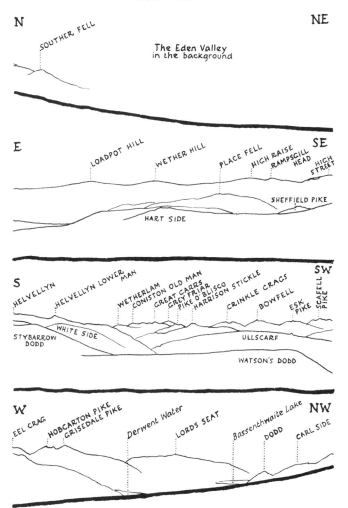

THE VIEW

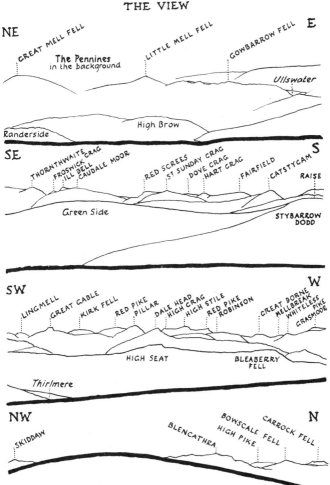

NOTES : This is the view from the shelter cairn,
not from the higher ground to the north.
Thirlmere, Derwent Water and Bassenthwaite Lake
cannot actually be seen from this point, but come
into view a few yards to the west.

Great Mell Fell
1760'

from Great Meldrum

Troutbeck
Penruddock

GREAT ▲ MELL FELL

▲ LITTLE
MELL
FELL

Matterdale End

▲ GOWBARROW
FELL

Dockray

MILES
0 1 2 3 4

Great Mell Fell is a prominent object on the Penrith approach to Lakeland. With its lesser twin, Little Mell Fell, it forms the portals to the Helvellyn range on this side. Its round 'inverted pudding-basin' shape does not promise much for the walker and it is rarely climbed. On closer acquaintance, however, it is rather more enjoyable than its appearance suggests, because of the presence of fine woodlands on the lower slopes; indeed, pines and larches persist almost to the summit. (Closer acquaintance was once frowned upon by the military authorities, but not any longer.)

NATURAL FEATURES

Great Mell Fell rises sharply from a wide expanse of desolate marshland to the north and west, territory not at all typical of Lakeland, the fell itself being much more fertile and colourful than its surroundings. Its rich red soil carries a wealth of timber, the eastern slopes especially being beautifully wooded. Bleached skeletons of trees near the top of the fell indicate that at one time it was more fully clothed; many of those that yet survive are battered by the prevailing wind into grotesque shapes.

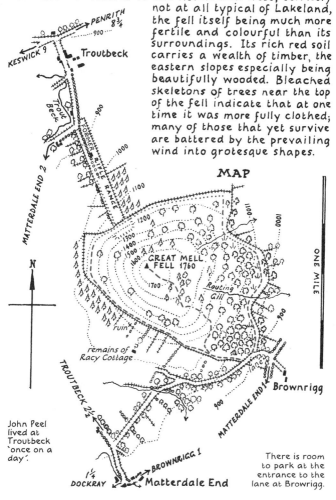

MAP

John Peel lived at Troutbeck 'once on a day'.

There is room to park at the entrance to the lane at Browrigg.

ASCENTS

Above the 1100' contour, roughly, the fell is enclosed within a fence. Access may be gained at Troutbeck (along a muddy lane) and at two gates at the southeastern corner. The danger signs that formerly guarded the entrances have been replaced by National Trust signs proclaiming this to be Mell Fell without the 'Great'.

An intermittent path makes a circuit of the fell inside the fence and it may be left anywhere for the climb to the top, but it is best to use the path that ascends the fell from the south-east. At one time the peripheral path gave a pleasant walk, but now much of it has gone out of use, and it is no longer recommended.

THE SUMMIT

Bilberries interspersed with cotton grass cover the level top. The decayed tree-trunk in the illustration has gone, and the few stones on the summit have been made into a cairn. The highest tree is still recognisable, although it has twisted a bit and put on some growth. The low mound on the summit is a tumulus.

DESCENTS: If Troutbeck is your destination, aim for the parallel fences of the former rifle range. Otherwise follow the path.

the highest tree

THE VIEW

The highlight of the view is Blencathra undoubtedly, the noble proportions of this fine mountain being seen to great advantage. Otherwise the panorama is uneven, with a wide expanse of the Eden Valley, an impressive grouping of fells southwards, and a vista of the Grasmoor range in the west.

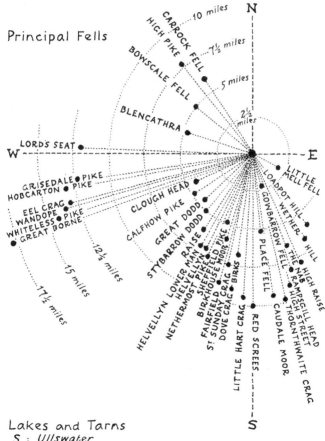

Principal Fells

Lakes and Tarns

S : Ullswater

(a disappointing view, only a very small section being visible)

Great Rigg

2513'

▲ FAIRFIELD

▲ GREAT
RIGG

▲ STONE ARTHUR

▲ HERON PIKE

• Grasmere ▲ NAB SCAR

• Rydal

Ambleside •

MILES
0 1 2 3 4

from Grasmere

NATURAL FEATURES

Great Rigg has no topographical secrets or surprises. It is a plain, straightforward, uninteresting fell on the southern spur of Fairfield, with gentle declivities linking the summit to the continuing ridge on either side. East, stony slopes fall abruptly to Rydal Beck; ruined crags rise from wastes of scree. To the west the fellside is mainly grassy but there are occasional rocks low down on this flank, above Tongue Gill. From the ridge south of the summit a descending shoulder strikes off in the direction of Grasmere; this has a rocky terminus with the name of Stone Arthur. Between the shoulder and the ridge is a deep, narrow trough which carries Greenhead Gill, Great Rigg's only stream of note, down to the River Rothay.

Few people will climb Great Rigg without also ascending Fairfield, for the former is a stepping-stone to its bigger neighbour. Whilst providing this humble service, however, the fell manages to retain a certain dignity, appreciated best from the west shore of Grasmere: seen from there, the dark dome of its summit appears to overtop all else.

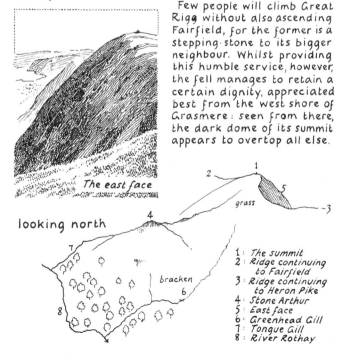

The east face

looking north

grass

bracken

1 : The summit
2 : Ridge continuing to Fairfield
3 : Ridge continuing to Heron Pike
4 : Stone Arthur
5 : East face
6 : Greenhead Gill
7 : Tongue Gill
8 : River Rothay

MAP

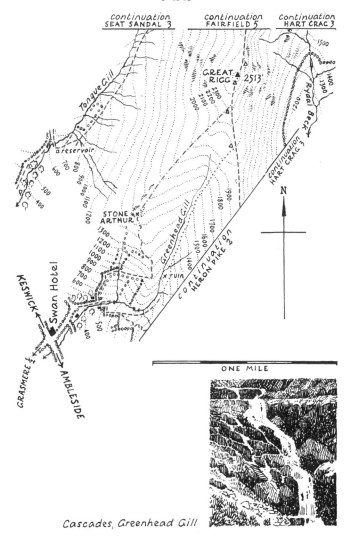

continuation
SEAT SANDAL 3

continuation
FAIRFIELD 5

continuation
HART CRAG 3

1500

1400

1300

Tongue Gill

GREAT
RIGG ▲ 2513

2300
2200
2100
2000

Rydal Beck

1200

reservoir

700
600
900
1000
1100
1200

continuation
HART CRAG 3

800

500

400

STONE
ARTHUR ✕

1900

1300
1200
1100
1000
900
800
700
600

Greenhead Gill

1800

1700

1600

1500

1400

continuation
HERON PIKE 2

N

KESWICK

Swan Hotel

ruin ✕

500

GRASMERE ½

400

AMBLESIDE

ONE MILE

Cascades, Greenhead Gill

ASCENT FROM GRASMERE
2300 feet of ascent : 3 miles

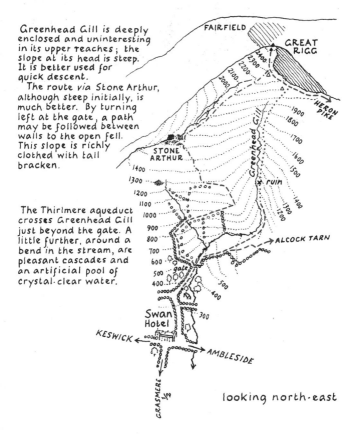

Greenhead Gill is deeply enclosed and uninteresting in its upper reaches; the slope at its head is steep. It is better used for quick descent.

The route *via* Stone Arthur, although steep initially, is much better. By turning left at the gate, a path may be followed between walls to the open fell. This slope is richly clothed with tall bracken.

The Thirlmere aqueduct crosses Greenhead Gill just beyond the gate. A little further, around a bend in the stream, are pleasant cascades and an artificial pool of crystal-clear water.

FAIRFIELD

GREAT RIGG

2400
2300
2200
2100
2000
1900
HERON PIKE
1800
1700
STONE ARTHUR
1600
1400
1500
1300
+ ruin
1200
1400
1100
1300
1000
1200
900
800
ALCOCK TARN
700
600
gate
500
500
400
400
300

Swan Hotel

KESWICK ←

← AMBLESIDE

GRASMERE 1/2

looking north-east

Great Rigg is more often visited on the tour of the Fairfield Horseshoe, but it may be ascended directly from Grasmere by the routes illustrated, that by Stone Arthur being the more interesting.

THE SUMMIT

Helvellyn   Fairfield

The summit is comprehended at a glance. A well-constructed symmetrical cairn occupies the highest point and another is 60 yards south, where the ridge steepens on its descent to Heron Pike. The top is a carpet of excellent turf which many a cricket-ground would welcome

RIDGE ROUTES

To FAIRFIELD, 2863' : 1 mile : N
Depression at 2375' : 500 feet of ascent
  An easy climb, needing care in mist
A fair path, on grass, crosses the depression but peters out as the summit is approached. Strangers to Fairfield should avoid it in mist.

To HERON PIKE, 2008' : 1½ miles
          SSW, then S
Minor depressions : 150 feet of ascent
A very easy high-level walk. Heron Pike is the *second* prominent rise on the ridge.

To STONE ARTHUR, 1652'
1¼ miles : SSW then SW
   Downhill all the way
Follow the wide grass shoulder branching from the main ridge. There is a path all the way.

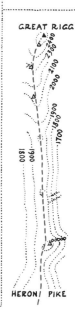

THE VIEW

The panorama is interesting and varied, a special feature being the large number of lakes and tarns in view. To the west, the mountain skyline is fine and there is an impressive vista of the Helvellyn group above the deep notch of Grisedale Hause

Principal Fells

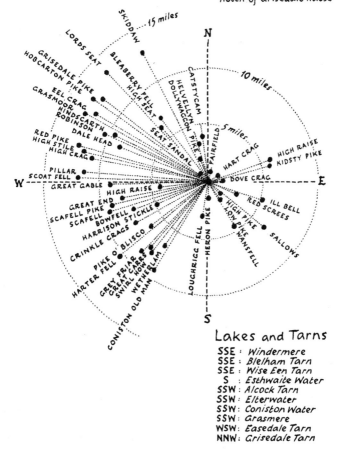

Lakes and Tarns

SSE : *Windermere*
SSE : *Blelham Tarn*
SSE : *Wise Een Tarn*
S : *Esthwaite Water*
SSW: *Alcock Tarn*
SSW: *Elterwater*
SSW: *Coniston Water*
SSW: *Grasmere*
WSW: *Easedale Tarn*
NNW: *Grisedale Tarn*

Hart Crag

2698'

Patterdale ●

Hartsop ●

FAIRFIELD ▲
HART ▲ CRAG
DOVE CRAG ▲

RED SCREES ▲

● Grasmere

● Rydal
Ambleside ●

MILES

0   1   2   3   4

from Dovedale

NATURAL FEATURES

Midway along the high-level traverse between Fairfield and Dove Crag is the rough top of Hart Crag, occupying a strategic position overlooking three valleys. To the north-east, Hart Crag follows usual mountain structure by sending out a long declining ridge, which forms a high barrier between desolate Deepdale and delectable Dovedale. North, a wall of crags defends the summit above the wild hollow of Link Cove, a hanging valley encompassed by cliffs: this is its finest aspect by far. South-west, after an initial fringe of broken crags, long stony slopes fall very steeply to Rydal Head. Although bounded by streams, Hart Crag itself is quite curiously deficient in water-courses.

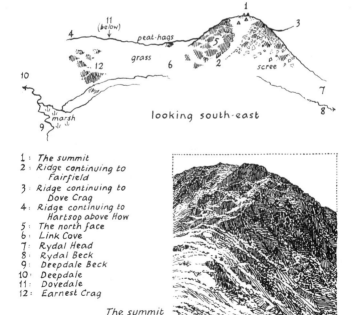

looking south-east

1 : The summit
2 : Ridge continuing to Fairfield
3 : Ridge continuing to Dove Crag
4 : Ridge continuing to Hartsop above How
5 : The north face
6 : Link Cove
7 : Rydal Head
8 : Rydal Beck
9 : Deepdale Beck
10 : Deepdale
11 : Dovedale
12 : Earnest Crag

The summit
from the northeast

MAP

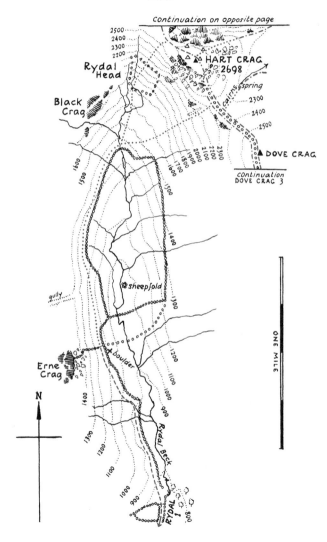

Continuation on opposite page

2500
2400
2300
2200

Rydal
Head

Black
Crag

HART CRAG
2698

cairn spring

2300
2400
2500

DOVE CRAG

continuation
DOVE CRAG 3

1600

1500

1800
2000
2100
2200
2300

1800
1700
1600

1500

1400

sheepfold

1300

1200

1100

1000

900

gully

ONE MILE

Erne
Crag

boulder

N

1400

1300

1200

1100

1000

Rydal Beck

RYDAL
900
800

MAP

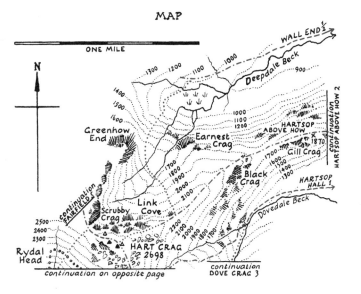

ONE MILE

N

Wall End ½
Deepdale Beck
900
Continuation HARTSOP ABOVE HOW 2
Greenhow End
Earnest Crag
1000
1100
1200
HARTSOP ABOVE HOW
Gill Crag
1870
1700
1600
1500
1400
1300
Black Crag
HARTSOP HALL 1
Scrubby Crag
Link Cove
Dovedale Beck
continuation FAIRFIELD
2500
2400
2300
Rydal Head
HART CRAG 2698
continuation on opposite page
continuation DOVE CRAG 3

The north face

ASCENT FROM RYDAL
2,600 feet of ascent : 4½ miles

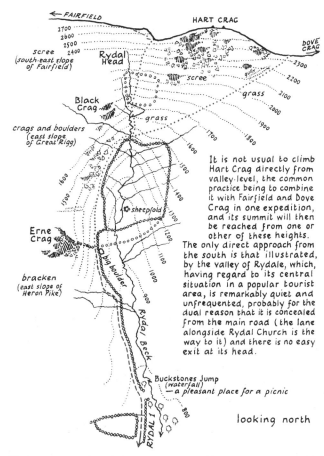

← FAIRFIELD

HART CRAG

2700
2600
2500
2400

scree
(south-east slope
of Fairfield)

Rydal
Head

DOVE
CRAG

2300

scree

2200

grass

2100

Black
Crag

2000

grass

1900

crags and boulders
(east slope
of Great Rigg)

1800

1700

1600

1500

1400

sheepfold

1300

Erne
Crag

1200

big boulder

1100

bracken
(east slope of
Heron Pike)

1000

Rydal Beck

900

RYDAL 1

Buckstones Jump
(waterfall)
— a pleasant place for a picnic

800

looking north

It is not usual to climb
Hart Crag directly from
valley-level, the common
practice being to combine
it with Fairfield and Dove
Crag in one expedition,
and its summit will then
be reached from one or
other of these heights.
The only direct approach from
the south is that illustrated,
by the valley of Rydale, which,
having regard to its central
situation in a popular tourist
area, is remarkably quiet and
unfrequented, probably for the
dual reason that it is concealed
from the main road (the lane
alongside Rydal Church is the
way to it) and there is no easy
exit at its head.

The approach by the Rydal Valley (Rydale) is attractive
and interesting, but the climb out of it is very steep. The
valley lies entirely within the circuit of the 'Fairfield
Horseshoe' and is deeply enclosed.

ASCENT FROM PATTERDALE
2,300 feet of ascent : 4½ miles from Patterdale village

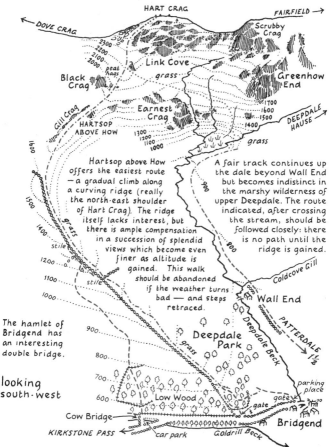

HART CRAG

FAIRFIELD →

← DOVE CRAG

Scrubby Crag

2300
2200
2100
2000
peat hags

Link Cove

grass

Black Crag

Greenhow End

Gill Crag

Earnest Crag

1700
1600
1500

DEEPDALE HAUSE →

HARTSOP ABOVE HOW

1300
1200
1100
1000

1400

1600

grass

Hartsop above How offers the easiest route — a gradual climb along a curving ridge (really the north-east shoulder of Hart Crag). The ridge itself lacks interest, but there is ample compensation in a succession of splendid views which become even finer as altitude is gained. This walk should be abandoned if the weather turns bad — and steps retraced.

A fair track continues up the dale beyond Wall End but becomes indistinct in the marshy wilderness of upper Deepdale. The route indicated, after crossing the stream, should be followed closely: there is no path until the ridge is gained.

1500

900

900

Coldcove Gill

1400

grass

stile

1200

stile

1100

1000

Wall End

PATTERDALE 1½ →

The hamlet of Bridgend has an interesting double bridge.

900

800

looking south-west

700

600

Deepdale Park

grass

Deepdale Beck

Low Wood

parking place

gate

gate

Cow Bridge

Bridgend

KIRKSTONE PASS

car park

Goldrill Beck

The ascent from Patterdale is far superior to that from the south. The Link Cove route especially is an interesting climb through the inner sanctuary of Hart Crag, the scene being impressive, but it is quite unsuitable in bad weather.

THE SUMMIT

The summit area is relatively small, its level top being about 120 yards long and having a cairn at each end. Two other cairns indicate viewpoints. The top is stony but a strip of grass running lengthwise across it to the north of the main cairns offers an easy traverse

Link Cove

FAIRFIELD

Col

grass

RYDALE (no path)

crags

2400

2500

2600

2698

boulders

HARTSOP ABOVE HOW (in clear weather only)

N

DOVEDALE (in clear weather only)

Col

RYDALE (no path)

DOVE CRAG

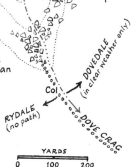

DESCENTS:
For Patterdale direct, the best way down in good weather is by the long ridge of Hartsop above How: an easy grass descent. The Link Cove route has no merit as a way off. For Rydal direct, the easier route is to descend from the depression between Hart Crag and Dove Crag, the slope here being less steep than that below the Fairfield - Hart Crag col.

Hart Crag can be a dangerous place in mist, the path across the summit being indistinct. Attempts to descend to Link Cove should not be considered. In emergency, aim for the depression between Hart Crag and Dove Crag. A safe descent from here may be made to Rydale, and, with care, to Dovedale. The wall is a safe guide to Ambleside.

YARDS

0   100   200

THE VIEW

Hart Crag is a little too near to the great mass of Fairfield to provide a well-balanced view. The panorama in other directions is extensive, but the picture as a whole is disappointing.

Principal Fells

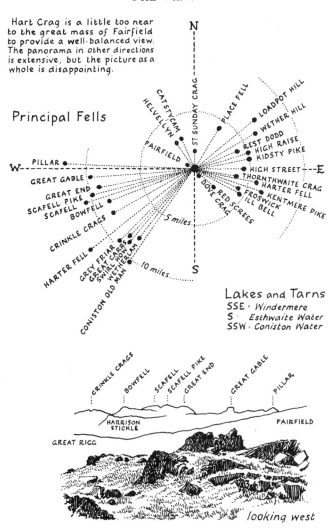

N

CATSTYCAM
HELVELLYN
ST SUNDAY CRAG
FAIRFIELD
PLACE FELL
LOADPOT HILL
WETHER HILL
REST DODD
HIGH RAISE
KIDSTY PIKE

W — PILLAR
GREAT GABLE
GREAT END
SCAFELL PIKE
SCAFELL
BOWFELL
CRINKLE CRAGS
HARTER FELL
GREY FRIAR
GREAT CARRS
SWIRL HOW
WETHERLAM
CONISTON OLD MAN

HIGH STREET — E
THORNTHWAITE CRAG
HARTER FELL
KENTMERE PIKE
FROSWICK
ILL BELL
RED SCREES
DOVE CRAG

5 miles

10 miles

S

Lakes and Tarns
SSE : Windermere
S : Esthwaite Water
SSW : Coniston Water

CRINKLE CRAGS
BOWFELL
SCAFELL
SCAFELL PIKE
GREAT END
GREAT GABLE
PILLAR

HARRISON STICKLE
FAIRFIELD

GREAT RIGG

looking west

RIDGE ROUTES

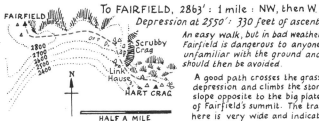

To FAIRFIELD, 2863': 1 mile : NW, then W.
Depression at 2550': 330 feet of ascent

An easy walk, but in bad weather Fairfield is dangerous to anyone unfamiliar with the ground and should then be avoided.

A good path crosses the grassy depression and climbs the stony slope opposite to the big plateau of Fairfield's summit. The track here is very wide and indicated by many cairns; excellent turf.

To DOVE CRAG, 2598': ¾ mile : SE.
Depression at 2350': 260 feet of ascent

An easy walk. Dove Crag is safe in mist, but care is then necessary in leaving Hart Crag.

An indistinct path, at first over grass and then, more clearly, among stones goes south from the eastern cairn to the wall at the depression. This wall continues over the summit of Dove Crag

To HARTSOP ABOVE HOW, 1870': 1½ miles : ENE
Depression at 1775': 150 feet of ascent

An easy walk. In mist the correct way off Hart Crag is not easy to find (there is no path) and this walk should not then be attempted.

Leave the summit near the main cairn, going down a patch of grass and crossing a band of scree before inclining slightly right down a shallow stony gully. Then work left to the ridge, which is broad and grassy, with many undulations and peat-hags. It narrows on the final rise.

Note that this ridge may be safely left *only* between Black Crag and Gill Crag (by descending right, to Dovedale)

ONE MILE

from the east ridge, St Sunday Crag

Hart Side

2481'

GREAT
DODD ▲   ● Dockray

▲ HART SIDE

STYBARROW ● Glencoyne
DODD ▲

● Glenridding

MILES

0   1   2   3

from Dockray

NATURAL FEATURES

The main watershed at Stybarrow Dodd sends out a long spur to the east which curves north from the subsidiary height of Green Side and continues at an elevated level until it is poised high above Ullswater before descending in wide slopes to the open country around Dockray. The principal height on this spur is Hart Side, which with its many satellites on the declining ridge forms the southern wall of the long valley of Deepdale throughout its sinuous course, its opposite boundary being the short deep trench of Glencoyne. The upper slopes of this bulky mass are unattractive in themselves, but, in strong contrast, the steep flank overlooking Ullswater is beautifully wooded, while the views of the lake from the Brown Hills, midway along the ridge, are of high quality.

Hart Side is rarely visited. Its smooth slopes, grass and marsh intermingling, seem very very remote from industry, but there are evidences that men laboured on these lonely heights a long time ago, and until 1962 the minerals far below its surface were being won by the enterprising miners of Glenridding.

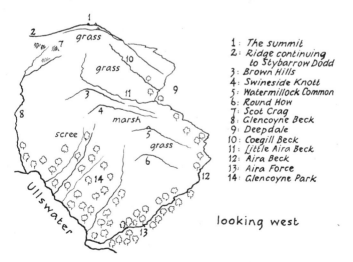

1: The summit
2: Ridge continuing to Stybarrow Dodd
3: Brown Hills
4: Swineside Knott
5: Watermillock Common
6: Round How
7: Scot Crag
8: Glencoyne Beck
9: Deepdale
10: Coegill Beck
11: Little Aira Beck
12: Aira Beck
13: Aira Force
14: Glencoyne Park

looking west

MAP

ONE MILE

When entering the area from Dowthwaitehead
turn left just before the end of the metalled road.
After passing the last building turn right, and
then left over the footbridge. After crossing the
bridge bear right through a wicket gate.

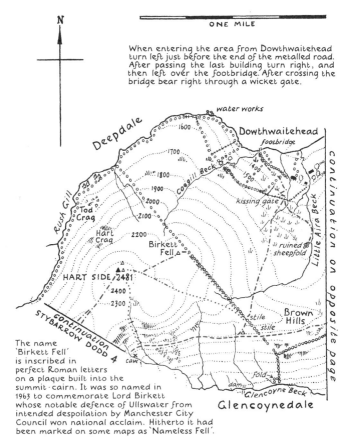

The name
'Birkett Fell'
is inscribed in
perfect Roman letters
on a plaque built into the
summit-cairn. It was so named in
1963 to commemorate Lord Birkett
whose notable defence of Ullswater from
intended despoilation by Manchester City
Council won national acclaim. Hitherto it had
been marked on some maps as 'Nameless Fell'.

According to the Ordnance Survey and Bartholomew's maps, the
representation of a footpath thereon is no evidence of a right of
way. Nor, unfortunately, is it evidence that a footpath now exists
at all! Some of the paths marked on those maps in the district
of Hart Side were made originally by miners on their way to or
from work at the Glenridding lead mine, but the miners now use
them no more: some paths have become overgrown and cannot
always be traced; others are starting to reappear.

MAP

continuation on opposite page

TROUTBECK 3

Dockray

Pounder Sike

Round How

quarry

stile

Park Brow

Aira Beck

Common Fell

Watermillock
Common

900

800

700

café

Little Aira Beck

fold

Swineside
Knott

Glencoyne
Park

stile

Brown
Hills

x fold

1500

1400

1300

1200

1000

900

800

700

600

Ullswater

Glencoyne Beck   Glencoyne

GLENRIDDING 1

N

ONE MILE

ASCENT FROM DOCKRAY
1600 feet of ascent : 4 miles

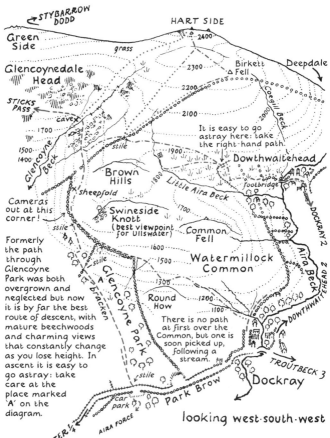

→ STYBARROW DODD

Green Side

HART SIDE
2400

Glencoynedale Head

grass

2300

Birkett △ Fell

Deepdale →

STICKS PASS

cave ×

2200

2100

Coalgill Beck

2000

1700

1500
1400

Glencoyne Beck

stile

1900

It is easy to go astray here: take the right-hand path

Dowthwaitehead

Brown Hills

× sheepfold

Little Aira Beck

footbridge

1800

DOCKRAY 2

Cameras out at this corner!

stile

Swineside Knott
(best viewpoint for Ullswater)

1700

Common Fell

Formerly the path through Glencoyne Park was both overgrown and neglected but now it is by far the best route of descent, with mature beechwoods and charming views that constantly change as you lose height. In ascent it is easy to go astray: take care at the place marked 'A' on the diagram.

stile

Glencoyne Park

bracken

stile

1600

1500

1300

1200

1100

Watermillock Common

Round How

There is no path at first over the Common, but one is soon picked up, following a stream.

Aira Beck

DOWTHWAITEHEAD 2

stile

car park

Park Brow

AIRA FORCE

ULLSWATER ½

TROUTBECK 3

Dockray

looking west·south·west

The joy of this walk is not to be found in the summit of Hart Side, which is dull, but in the splendid high-level route to it from Dockray, which excels in views of Ullswater. The Dowthwaitehead route deserves no consideration.

THE SUMMIT

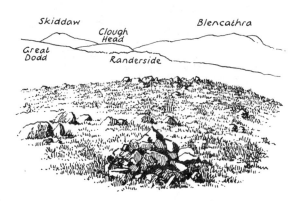

The summit has nothing extraordinary to show in natural forms, being grassy with a few outcropping boulders. Yet this is a top that cannot be confused with any other, for here man has not contented himself merely with building a few cairns but has really got to work with pick and spade, and excavated a most remarkable ditch, rather like the Vallum of the Roman Wall. As the project was abandoned, the reason for the prodigious effort is not clear. An excavation below the summit, intended as the site of a building, has now been smoothed out. Probably these were workings for the Glenridding lead mine, as is a cave in Glencoynedale Head, near the miners' path; the key to its location is the spoil heap just below it. The cave entrance is smaller than it was when it was illustrated here.

The ditch on the summit

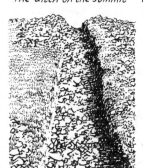

DESCENTS : Descents will usually be either to Dockray or Glencoyne. Walk ESE, over a minor rise, to the wall running across the fell. Follow the wall down, joining the miners' path (at a gap) for Dockray. For Glencoyne, continue by the wall down into the valley. These are the best routes in mist.

The cave

RIDGE ROUTE

To STYBARROW DODD, 2770'
1½ miles: SW then W
Depressions at 2250' and 2525'
550 feet of ascent

An easy walk on grass. Safe in mist.
Follow round the head of Deepdale,
skirting the intermediate summit
of Green Side. In mist, take care
to keep the rising slope on the left.

Ullswater, from the Brown Hills

THE VIEW

Principal Fells

The view is disappointing. Although Hart Side has a considerable altitude, it does not overtop the main ridge to the west, which hides all the high fells beyond. Intervening ground to the east conceals most of Ullswater.

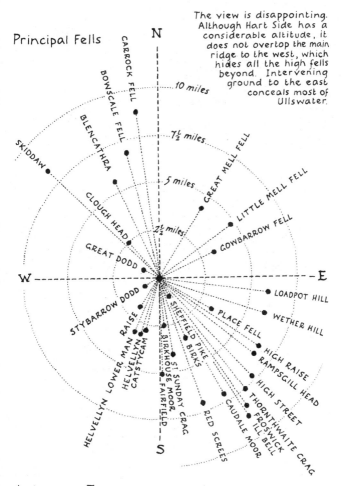

N

10 miles
7½ miles
5 miles
2½ miles

CARROCK FELL
BOWSCALE FELL
BLENCATHRA
SKIDDAW
CLOUGH HEAD
GREAT DODD
GREAT MELL FELL
LITTLE MELL FELL
COWBARROW FELL

W ——— E

STYBARROW DODD
RAISE
LOWER MAN
HELVELLYN
CATSTYCAM
HELVELLYN
SHEFFIELD PIKE
BIRKHOUSE MOOR
BIRKS
ST SUNDAY CRAG
FAIRFIELD
RED SCREES
CAUDALE MOOR
ILL BELL
FROSWICK
THORNTHWAITE CRAG
HIGH STREET
RAMPSGILL HEAD
HIGH RAISE
WETHER HILL
LOADPOT HILL
PLACE FELL

S

Lakes and Tarns
ENE : *Ullswater*

Hartsop above How

1870'

The 2002 edition of the 2½-inch O.S. map
shows a 580-metre contour, making
the altitude slightly greater
than 1900 feet, but gives
no spot height.

from Hunsett Cove

Patterdale •

St SUNDAY ▲   Hartsop
CRAG   •

FAIRFIELD   ▲ HARTSOP
▲   ABOVE HOW

HART CRAG
          ▲ DOVE CRAG

MILES
0   1   2   3

The long curving northeast ridge of Hart
Crag rises to a separate summit midway,
and this summit is generally referred to as
Hartsop above How by guidebook writers
and mapmakers. Sometimes the three words
in the name are hyphenated, sometimes not.
Probably the first two should be, but not the
last two: the word 'How' is common, meaning
a low hill, and the distinctive title of this
particular How is 'Hartsop-above', indicating
its geographical relationship to the hamlet
in the valley below. Most natives of Deepdale,
however, know it not by this name, with or
without hyphens, but they all know Gill Crag,
which fringes the summit, and this would
seem to be a more satisfactory name for the fell. But one cannot
so wantonly ignore the authority of the guidebooks and maps; and
the name Hartsop above How, without hyphens (in the belief that
an error of omission is a less sin than an error of commission) will
be used here in support of the Director General of Ordnance Survey.

NATURAL FEATURES

Hartsop above How is a simple ridge (really a part of Hart Crag) curving like a sickle to enclose the valley of Deepdale on the south and east. Only in the vicinity of the summit is it at all narrow, but both flanks are steep throughout most of its three-mile length, the slopes above Dovedale being especially rough. There are several crags on the fell, the most imposing being Black Crag above the rough hollow of Hunsett Cove; also prominent are the grey rocks of Dovedale Slabs (looking as pleasant and attractive as steep rocks can look) below the eastern end of the summit, and, on the Deepdale side, the gloomy cliff of Earnest Crag (looking as unpleasant and unattractive as steep rocks can look). The slopes above Brothers Water are well-wooded over an extensive area, and Deepdale Park also has some fine trees.

N

MAP

PATTERDALE 1

parking place

Bridgend

gate

Goldrill Beck

Wall End

Deepdale Park

car park

Deepdale Beck

700
800
900
1000
1100
1200

stile

HARTSOP ½

Low Wood

Deepdale

stile

Brothers Water

1300
1400
1500
1600

Kirkstone Beck

HARTSOP ABOVE HOW

1700
1800
1870
Dovedale Slabs

Gill Crag

Hartsop Hall

SYKESIDE CAMPSITE

continuation HART CRAG 4

Black Crag

mine

Dove Falls

Dovedale

Dovedale Beck

HALF A MILE

ASCENT FROM PATTERDALE
1400 feet of ascent : 3 miles from Patterdale village

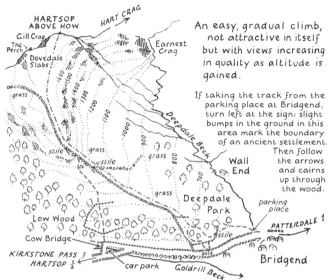

An easy, gradual climb, not attractive in itself but with views increasing in quality as altitude is gained.

If taking the track from the parking place at Bridgend, turn left at the sign: slight bumps in the ground in this area mark the boundary of an ancient settlement. Then follow the arrows and cairns up through the wood.

looking south·west

Dovedale Slabs

THE SUMMIT

The highest point is a grassy knoll adjoining the top of a cleft splitting Gill Crag, but the usually accepted summit is 200 yards northeast.

DESCENTS : The easiest way down *in any conditions* is by the ridge to the road. Direct descents, either to Deepdale or Dovedale, are too rough.

THE VIEW

There is no better place for appraising the ruggedness of the eastern crags and coves of the Fairfield group of fells

Principal Fells :

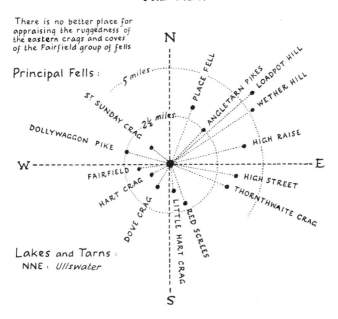

N

5 miles

2½ miles

PLACE FELL
ANGLETARN PIKES
LOADPOT HILL
WETHER HILL
ST SUNDAY CRAG
DOLLYWAGGON PIKE
HIGH RAISE
FAIRFIELD
HIGH STREET
HART CRAG
THORNTHWAITE CRAG
DOVE CRAG
RED SCREES
LITTLE HART CRAG

W — — — — — — — E

S

Lakes and Tarns :
NNE : *Ullswater*

RIDGE ROUTE

To HART CRAG, 2698′ : 1½ miles : WSW
Depression at 1775′ : 1000 feet of ascent
An easy walk on grass at first, then
a rough scramble. No path.
Dangerous in mist.
Continue along the ridge
to a grassy depression,
then directly ahead.

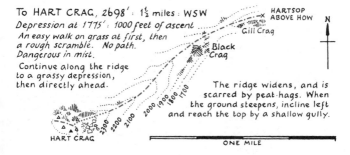

HARTSOP
ABOVE HOW
Gill Crag
Black
Crag

N

The ridge widens, and is
scarred by peat-hags. When
the ground steepens, incline left
and reach the top by a shallow gully.

2300 2200 2100 2000 1900 1800 1700

HART CRAG

ONE MILE

Helvellyn

3118'

from the south-west ridge of St *Sunday Crag*

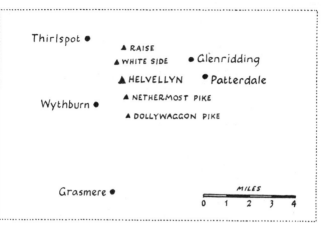

Thirlspot ●
▲ RAISE
▲ WHITE SIDE   ● Glenridding
▲ HELVELLYN   ● Patterdale
▲ NETHERMOST PIKE
Wythburn ●
▲ DOLLYWAGGON PIKE

Grasmere ●   MILES
                              0   1   2   3   4

   Legend and poetry, a lovely name and a lofty altitude
combine to encompass Helvellyn in an aura of romance; and
thousands of pilgrims, aided by its easy accessibility, are
attracted to its summit every year. There is no doubt that
Helvellyn is climbed more often than any other mountain
in Lakeland, and, more than any other, it is the objective
and ambition of the tourist who does not normally climb;
moreover, the easy paths leading up the western flanks
make it particularly suitable for sunrise expeditions, and,
in a snowy winter, its sweeping slopes afford great sport
to the ski parties who congregate on these white expanses.
There are few days in any year when no visitor calls at
the wall-shelter on the summit to eat his sandwiches. It
is a great pity that Helvellyn is usually ascended by its
western routes, for this side is unattractive and lacking
in interest. From the east, however, the approach is quite
exciting, with the reward of an extensive panorama as a
sudden and dramatic climax when the top is gained; only
to the traveller from this direction does Helvellyn display
its true character and reveal its secrets. There is some
quality about Helvellyn which endears it in the memory
of most people who have stood on its breezy top; although
it can be a grim place indeed on a wild night, it is, as a
rule, a very friendly giant. If it did not inspire affection
would its devotees return to it so often ?

NATURAL FEATURES

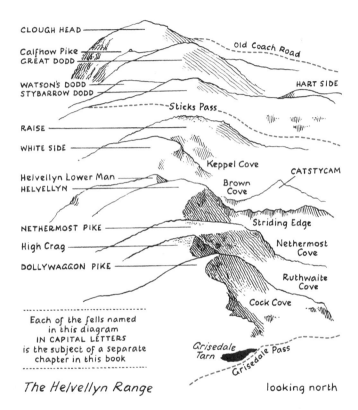

CLOUGH HEAD

Calfhow Pike
GREAT DODD

Old Coach Road

WATSON'S DODD
STYBARROW DODD

HART SIDE

Sticks Pass

RAISE

WHITE SIDE

Keppel Cove

CATSTYCAM

Helvellyn Lower Man
HELVELLYN

Brown
Cove

NETHERMOST PIKE

Striding Edge

High Crag

Nethermost
Cove

DOLLYWAGGON PIKE

Ruthwaite
Cove

Cock Cove

- - - - - - - - - - - - - - - -
Each of the fells named
in this diagram
IN CAPITAL LETTERS
is the subject of a separate
chapter in this book
- - - - - - - - - - - - - - - -

Grisedale
Tarn

Grisedale Pass

The Helvellyn Range

looking north

The altitude of these fells and the main connecting ridges
is consistently above 2500 feet from Dollywaggon Pike (2815')
to Great Dodd (2812') except for the depression of Sticks Pass,
which is slightly below. This is the greatest area of high fells
in Lakeland, and the traverse of the complete range from south
to north (the better way) is a challenge to all active walkers.
(As a preliminary canter, strong men will include the Fairfield group,
starting at Kirkstone Pass and reaching Grisedale Tarn over the tops
of Red Screes, Little Hart Crag, Dove Crag, Hart Crag and Fairfield)

NATURAL FEATURES

The Helvellyn range is extremely massive, forming a tremendous natural barrier from north to south between the deep troughs of the Thirlmere and Ullswater valleys. The many fells in this vast upland area are each given a separate chapter in this book, and the following notes relate only to Helvellyn itself, with its main summit at 3118' (the third highest in Lakeland) and a subsidiary at 3033'.

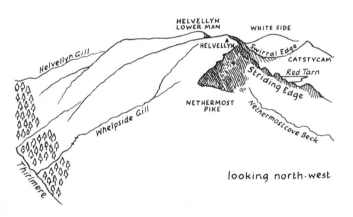

looking north·west

Helvellyn is a high point on a high ridge and therefore is substantially buttressed by neighbouring heights, the connecting depressions, north and south, being relatively slight. Westwards, however, after a gentle incline from the summit the slope quickens and finally plunges steeply down to Thirlmere, the total fall in height being nearly half a mile in a lateral distance of little more than one mile. This great mountain wall below the upper slopes is of simple design, consisting of two broad buttresses each bounded by swift·flowing streams and scarred by broken crags and occasional scree gullies. The base of the slope is densely planted with conifers.

continued

NATURAL FEATURES

continued

The smooth slopes curving up from the west break abruptly along the ridge, where, in complete contrast, a shattered cliff of crag and scree falls away precipitously eastwards : here are the most dramatic scenes Helvellyn has to offer. From the edge of the declivity on the summit Red Tarn is seen directly below, enclosed between the bony arms of Swirral Edge on the left and Striding Edge on the right. Swirral Edge terminates in the grassy cone of Catstycam, a graceful peak, but Striding Edge is all bare rock, a succession of jagged fangs ending in a black tower. The Edges are bounded by deep rough hollows, silent and very lonely. Beyond the Edges is the bulky mass of Birkhouse Moor, Helvellyn's long east shoulder, a high wedge separating Grisedale and Glenridding and descending to the lovely shores of Ullswater.

Striding Edge

Early writers regarded Striding Edge as a place of terror; contemporary writers, following a modern fashion, are inclined to dismiss it as of little account. In fact, Striding Edge is the finest ridge there is in Lakeland, for walkers — its traverse is always an exhilarating adventure in fair weather or foul, and it can be made easy or difficult according to choice. The danger of accident is present only when a high wind is blowing or when the rocks are iced : in a mist on a calm day, the Edge is a really fascinating place.

Swirral Edge

Helvellyn from Red Tarn

MAP

continuation on next page

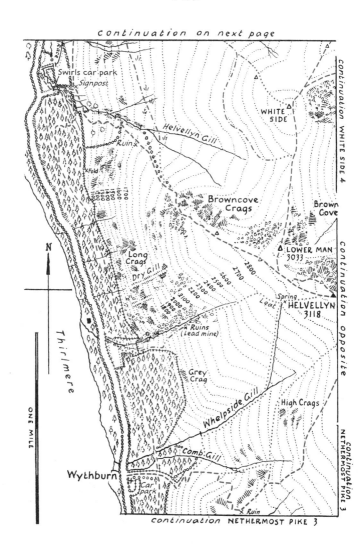

continuation WHITE SIDE 4

continuation opposite

continuation NETHERMOST PIKE 3

continuation NETHERMOST PIKE 3

MAP

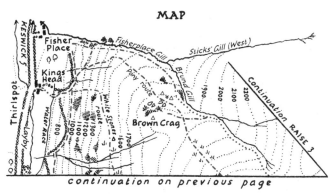

continuation on previous page

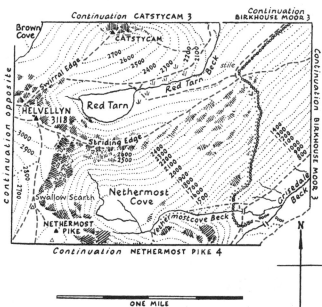

ONE MILE

THE WESTERN APPROACHES

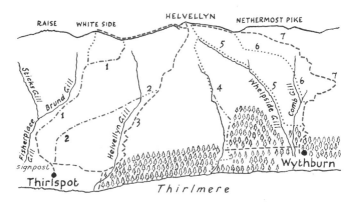

1 : **The old pony-route :** The original, longest and easiest route. The path is now becoming intermittent owing to disuse. This route is preferable to the Helvellyn Gill route because it avoids the crowds. It is hard to imagine ponies coming this way now.

2 : **The 'White Stones' route :** Once the usual and popular way up from Thirlspot, this route is now going out of use. To find it turn right at the signpost for fifty paces and head up the hill.

3 : *via* **Helvellyn Gill :** A very popular route, starting at the Swirls car park. The start is clearly signposted. Much of the steepness has been relieved by the construction of a zigzag path, and recent improvements eliminate the need to negotiate scree.

4 : *via* **the old lead mine :** The shortest way to the top from the road, taking advantage of a breach in the plantation. Very steep and rough for 2,200 feet. Solitary walkers with weak ankles should avoid this route: it is *not* recognised and is not attractive. It is linked to the car park at Wythburn by a forest road.

5 : *via* **Whelpside Gill :** A good route on a hot day, with water close almost to the summit. Rough scrambling in the gill. No path.

6 : *via* **Comb Gill :** A route of escape from the crowds on the popular Birk Side path. Steep up by the gill, but generally easy walking most of the way, on grass.

7 : **The 'Wythburn' route, via Birk Side :** One of the most popular ways up Helvellyn, and the usual route from Wythburn. Good path throughout. Steep for the first mile, then much easier.

These routes are illustrated on pages 11 and 12 following

THE WESTERN APPROACHES

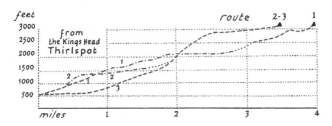

from the Kings Head
Thirlspot

route   2-3   1

feet
3000
2500
2000
1500
1000
500

miles   1   2   3   4

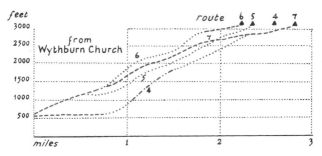

from
Wythburn Church

route   6 5   4   7

feet
3000
2500
2000
1500
1000
500

miles   1   2   3

Helvellyn Gill

In mist:

Route 1 is impossible to find in descent.

Route 2 is difficult to find in ascent and impossible to find in descent.

Route 3 is easy to find and easy to follow.

Route 4 is safe but seems even rougher in mist.

Route 5 is safe if the gill is kept alongside.

Route 6 is better avoided.

Route 7 is best of all, the path being distinct throughout its length.

Whelpside Gill

ASCENT FROM THIRLSPOT
2600 feet of ascent : 3½ - 4 miles

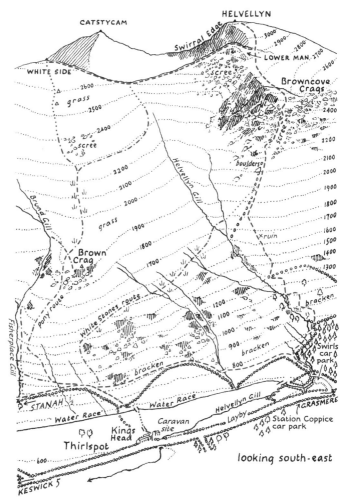

looking south-east

See Helvellyn 9 for details of the routes illustrated

ASCENT FROM WYTHBURN
2550 feet of ascent : 2¼ - 2¾ miles

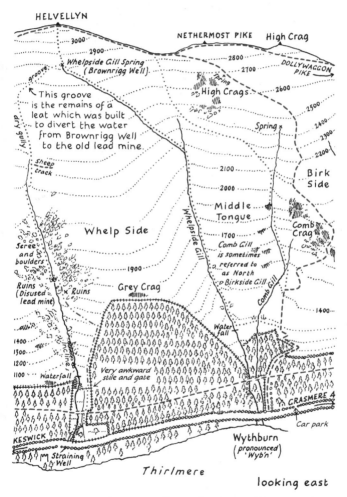

HELVELLYN

3000

NETHERMOST PIKE   High Crag

2900

Whelpside Gill Spring
(Brownrigg Well).   2800

DOLLYWAGGON
PIKE

2700

High Crags

groove

↖ This groove
is the remains of a
leat which was built
to divert the water
from Brownrigg Well
to the old lead mine.   2600

2500

Spring ×   2400

2300

2200

old leat

sheep
track

2100

Birk
Side

2000

1700

Middle
Tongue

Comb
Crag

Whelp Side

Whelpside Gill

Scree
and
boulders

1900

Comb Gill
is sometimes
referred to
as North
Birkside Gill

Ruins
(Disused
lead mine)   × Ruins   Grey Crag

Comb Gill

1400

1400
1300
1200
1100   Waterfall

Incline

Water
fall

Very awkward
stile and gate

GRASMERE 4

Car park

KESWICK

Straining
Well

Wythburn
(pronounced
'Wyb'n')

Thirlmere   looking east

See Helvellyn 9 for details of the routes illustrated

THE EASTERN APPROACHES

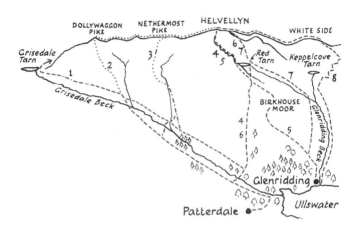

1 : *via* Grisedale Tarn : A long easy walk on a good path, with only one steep section. An interesting and pleasant route, which can be improved by following the edge of the escarpment between Dollywaggon Pike and the summit, instead of the path.

2 : *via* Ruthwaite Cove and Dollywaggon Pike : A very fine route for the more adventurous walker, cutting off a big corner of Route 1 – but the variation is steep and pathless.

3 : *via* Nethermost Cove and Nethermost Pike : A twin to Route 2, with a steep enjoyable scramble. Not for novices.

4 and 5 : *via* Striding Edge : The best ways of all, well known, popular, and often densely populated in summer. The big attraction is an airy rock ridge, very fine indeed. Good paths throughout.

6 : *via* Red Tarn and Swirral Edge, from Patterdale : An easier variation finish to Route 4, marshy by Red Tarn, ending in a good scramble up a steep rock staircase.

7 : *via* Red Tarn and Swirral Edge, from Glenridding : An easy walk finishing in a good scramble up a steep rock staircase.

8 : The old pony-route *via* Keppel Cove : The original route from Glenridding. A long but easy and interesting walk.

Routes 4, 6, 7 and 8 are illustrated on pages 15 and 16 following. For Routes 1, 2 and 3, the diagrams on Dollywaggon Pike 5 and 7 and Nethermost Pike 6, respectively, will be helpful. Further details of Route 5 are to be found on Birkhouse Moor 6.

THE EASTERN APPROACHES

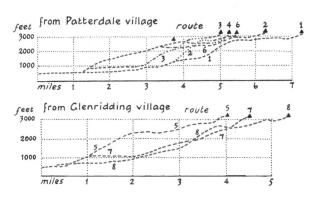

from Patterdale village   route

from Glenridding village   route

In mist :

Route 1 is easy to follow every inch of the way.
Routes 2 and 3 should be avoided absolutely.
Routes 4 and 5 are safe for anyone already familiar
   with them.

Route 6 is safe, but there will be uncertainty near Red Tarn.
Routes 7 and 8 are distinct all the way.

The summit, from Striding Edge

ASCENT FROM PATTERDALE
2700 feet of ascent : 5 miles

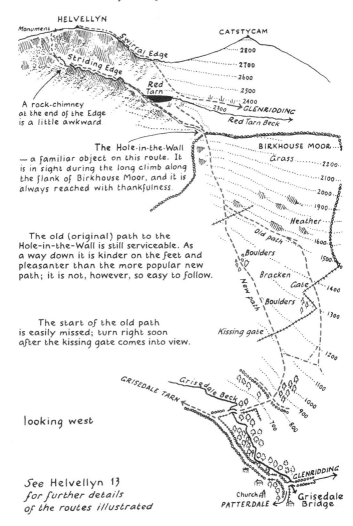

HELVELLYN

Monument

CATSTYCAM

Swirral Edge

Striding Edge

Red Tarn

A rock-chimney
at the end of the Edge
is a little awkward.

2800
2700
2600
2500
2400
2300 GLENRIDDING
Red Tarn Beck

The Hole-in-the-Wall
— a familiar object on this route. It
is in sight during the long climb along
the flank of Birkhouse Moor, and it is
always reached with thankfulness.

BIRKHOUSE MOOR

Grass

2200
2100
2000
1900

Heather

The old (original) path to the
Hole-in-the-Wall is still serviceable. As
a way down it is kinder on the feet and
pleasanter than the more popular new
path; it is not, however, so easy to follow.

Old path

1800

Boulders

1500

Bracken

Gate

1400

New path

Boulders

1300

The start of the old path
is easily missed; turn right soon
after the kissing gate comes into view.

Kissing gate

1200

1100

GRISEDALE TARN

Grisedale Beck

1000
900
700 800

looking west

See Helvellyn 13
for further details
of the routes illustrated

GLENRIDDING

Church
PATTERDALE

Grisedale
Bridge

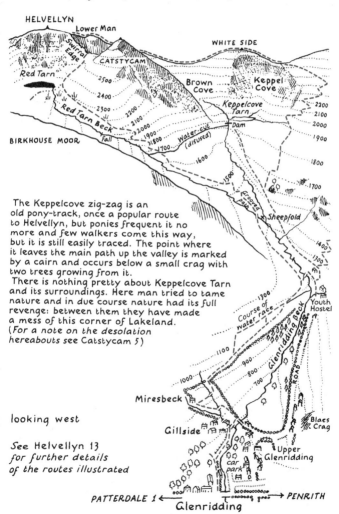

ASCENT FROM GLENRIDDING
2750 feet of ascent : 4½ or 5½ miles

HELVELLYN
Lower Man
Swirral Edge
CATSTYCAM
Red Tarn
WHITE SIDE
2500
2400
2300
2200
2100
Brown Cove
Keppel Cove
Keppelcove Tarn
Dam
2200
2100
2000
1900
Red Tarn Beck
Fall
2000
1800
1700
1600
Water-cut (disused)
BIRKHOUSE MOOR
1500
1800
1700
Grooved path
Sheepfold
1400
1300

The Keppelcove zig-zag is an
old pony-track, once a popular route
to Helvellyn, but ponies frequent it no
more and few walkers come this way,
but it is still easily traced. The point where
it leaves the main path up the valley is marked
by a cairn and occurs below a small crag with
two trees growing from it.
There is nothing pretty about Keppelcove Tarn
and its surroundings. Here man tried to tame
nature and in due course nature had its full
revenge: between them they have made
a mess of this corner of Lakeland.
(For a note on the desolation
hereabouts see Catstycam 5)

1300
Youth Hostel
1300
Course of water race
1100
Glenridding Beck
ROAD
1000
900
800
700

Miresbeck
Blaes Crag

looking west

Gillside

Upper Glenridding

See Helvellyn 13
for further details
of the routes illustrated

car park

PATTERDALE 1 ←   → PENRITH
Glenridding

ASCENT FROM GRASMERE
3050 feet of ascent : 6½ miles from Grasmere Church

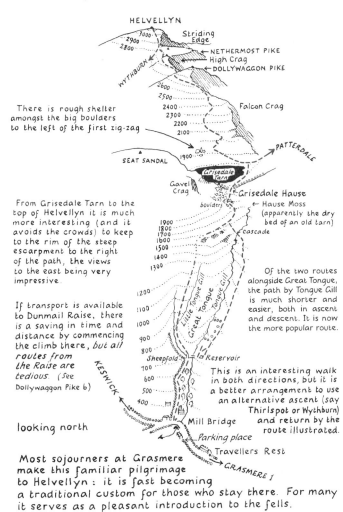

HELVELLYN

3000
2900
2800

WYTHBURN

Striding Edge

← NETHERMOST PIKE
High Crag
← DOLLYWAGGON PIKE

2600
2500

Falcon Crag

There is rough shelter amongst the big boulders to the left of the first zig-zag

2400
2300
2200
2100

1900

PATTERDALE

SEAT SANDAL

Grisedale Tarn

Gavel Crag

Grisedale Hause

boulders

← Hause Moss (apparently the dry bed of an old tarn)

From Grisedale Tarn to the top of Helvellyn it is much more interesting (and it avoids the crowds) to keep to the rim of the steep escarpment to the right of the path, the views to the east being very impressive.

1900
1800
1700
1600
1500
1400
1300

cascade

Of the two routes alongside Great Tongue, the path by Tongue Gill is much shorter and easier, both in ascent and descent. It is now the more popular route.

1200

1100

1000

900

800

Little Tongue Gill

Great Tongue

Tongue Gill

If transport is available to Dunmail Raise, there is a saving in time and distance by commencing the climb there, *but all routes from the Raise are tedious.* (See Dollywaggon Pike 6)

KESWICK

Sheepfold

Reservoir

700
600
500
400

This is an interesting walk in both directions, but it is a better arrangement to use an alternative ascent (say Thirlspot or Wythburn) and return by the route illustrated.

looking north

Mill Bridge

Parking place
Travellers Rest

GRASMERE 1

Most sojourners at Grasmere make this familiar pilgrimage to Helvellyn : it is fast becoming a traditional custom for those who stay there. For many it serves as a pleasant introduction to the fells.

Helvellyn Lower Man

looking northwest

Helvellyn Lower Man, half a mile northwest of the principal top, occupies a key position on the main ridge, which here changes its direction subtly and unobtrusively. Walkers intending to follow the ridge north may easily go astray hereabouts. The wide path from Helvellyn skirts the Lower Man and continues clearly along a broad spur which appears to be the main ridge, but is not (*this is the direct way to the car park at Swirls*).

Summit of Lower Man   HELVELLYN

Browncove Crags
— oddly named because Brown Cove is on the other side of the ridge.

THE SUMMIT

It might be expected that the summit of so popular a mountain would be crowned with a cairn the size of a house, instead of which the only adornment is a small and insignificant heap of stones that commands no respect at all, untidily thrown together on the mound forming the highest point. It is a disappointment to have no cairn to recline against, and as there is no natural seat anywhere on the top visitors inevitably drift into the nearby wall-shelter and there rest ankle-deep in the debris of countless packed lunches. The summit is covered in shale and is lacking in natural features, a deficiency which man has attempted to remedy by erecting thereon, as well as the shelter, a triangulation column and two monuments. And until many walkers learn better manners there is a crying need for an incinerator also, to dispose of the decaying heaps of litter they leave behind to greet those who follow.

The paths across the summit are wide and so well-trodden as to appear almost metalled: they are unnecessarily and amply cairned.

The dull surroundings are relieved by the exciting view down the escarpment to Red Tarn and Striding Edge below.

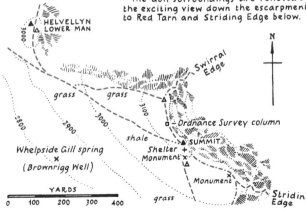

DESCENTS

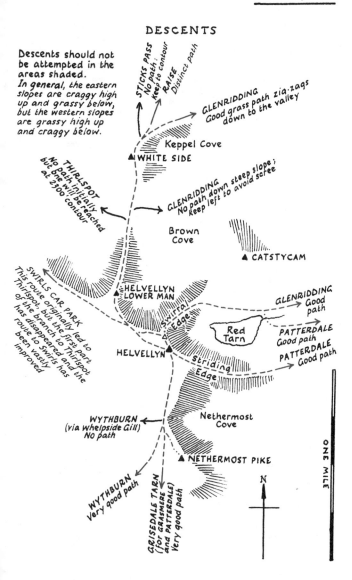

Descents should not
be attempted in the
areas shaded.
In general, the eastern
slopes are craggy high
up and grassy below,
but the western slopes
are grassy high up
and craggy below.

STICKS PASS
No path:
keep to contour

RAISE
Distinct path

GLENRIDDING
Good grass path zig-zags
down to the valley

Keppel Cove

▲ WHITE SIDE

THIRLSPOT
No path initially
but one will be reached
at 2300 contour

GLENRIDDING
No path down steep slope;
keep left to avoid scree

Brown
Cove

▲ CATSTYCAM

SWIRLS CAR PARK
This route originally led to
Thirlspot, but the first part
of the branch to Thirlspot
route has disappeared and the
route to Swirls has
been vastly
improved

▲ HELVELLYN
LOWER MAN

Swirral
Edge

Red
Tarn

GLENRIDDING
Good
path

PATTERDALE
Good path

PATTERDALE
Good path

△ HELVELLYN

Striding
Edge

WYTHBURN
(via Whelpside Gill)
No path

Nethermost
Cove

▲ NETHERMOST PIKE

N

WYTHBURN
Very good path

GRISEDALE TARN
(for Grasmere
and Patterdale)
Very good path

ONE MILE

RIDGE ROUTES

To HELVELLYN LOWER MAN, 3033': ½ mile : NW

Depression at 2975': 60 feet of ascent

A simple stroll, safe in mist.

Take the Thirlspot path, forking right below the cone of Lower Man. Or, better, follow the edge of the escarpment all the way.

NOTE : *Helvellyn Lower Man stands at the point where the main ridge makes an abrupt and unexpected right-angled turn. Its summit must be traversed for White Side, Sticks Pass or Glenridding.*

- -

To CATSTYCAM, 2917': 1 mile : NW (200 yards), then NE

Depression at 2600': 320 feet of ascent

A splendid walk with a fine rock scramble.
Safe in mist; dangerous in ice and snow.

200 yards north-west of the top of Helvellyn is a cairn (the Ordnance Survey column is midway), and just beyond, over the rim, is the start of the steep rock stairway going down to Swirral Edge: the descent is less formidable than it looks. Midway along the Edge the main path turns off to the right: here continue ahead up the grass slope to the summit.

- -

The Monuments of Helvellyn

The Gough Memorial

Erected 1890 on the edge of the summit above the path to Striding Edge.

This small stone tablet, 40 yards S of the shelter, commemorates the landing of an aeroplane in 1926. (Playful pedestrians may have hidden it with stones)

The Dixon Memorial 1858

Situated on a platform of rock on Striding Edge overlooking Nethermost Cove (often not noticed)

RIDGE ROUTES

To BIRKHOUSE MOOR, 2356′: 2 miles : ESE then NE
Minor depressions only : 100 feet of ascent

An unpleasant descent on loose scree, followed by an exhilarating scramble along a narrow rock ridge and an easy walk. Dangerous in snow and ice; care necessary in gusty wind ; safe in mist.

Turn down the scree for Striding Edge 30 yards beyond the monument. The Edge begins with a 20′ chimney, well furnished with holds : this is the only difficulty. From the rock tower at the far end the path slants across the slope but it is pleasanter to follow the crest.

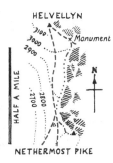

To NETHERMOST PIKE, 2920′
¾ mile : S then SE

Depression at 2840′ : 80 feet of ascent
A very easy walk. Safe in mist.

A broad path leads south to the depression known as Swallow Scarth. Here the path divides, one branch descending to Wythburn, and the other continuing over the flat top of Nethermost Pike. To visit the summit-cairn bear left at the fork, and left again in about fifty yards, along a faint path.

In clear weather a more interesting route follows the edge of the escarpment, the views being very impressive.

Whelpside Gill Spring (Brownrigg Well)

Few visitors to Helvellyn know of this spring (the source of Whelpside Gill), which offers unfailing supplies of icy water. To find it, walk 500 yards south of west from the top in the direction of Pillar.

THE VIEW

The figures following the names of fells
indicate distances in miles

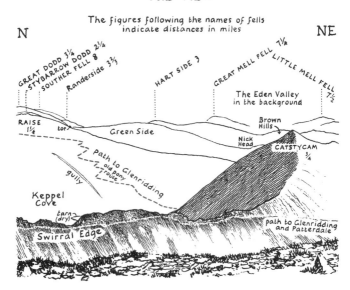

N — NE

GREAT DODD 3¼
STYBARROW DODD 2¼
SOUTHER FELL 8
Randerside 3⅔
HART SIDE 3
GREAT MELL FELL 7⅛
LITTLE MELL FELL 7½

The Eden Valley
in the background

RAISE
1¼
tor.
Green Side
Brown
Hills
Nick
Head
CATSTYCAM
¾

Path to Glenridding
old pony
route
gully

Keppel
Cove

Tarn
(dry)
Swirral Edge
path to Glenridding
and Patterdale

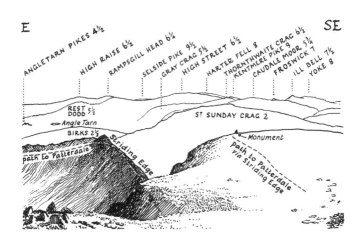

E — SE

ANGLETARN PIKES 4½
HIGH RAISE 6½
RAMPSGILL HEAD 6¼
SELSIDE PIKE 9½
GRAY CRAG 5½
HIGH STREET 6½
HARTER FELL 8
THORNTHWAITE CRAG 6½
KENTMERE PIKE 9
CAUDALE MOOR 5¾
FROSWICK 7
ILL BELL 7½
YOKE 8

REST
DODD 5½
Angle Tarn
BIRKS 2½
ST SUNDAY CRAG 2
Striding Edge
Monument
path to Patterdale
Path to Patterdale
via Striding Edge

THE VIEW

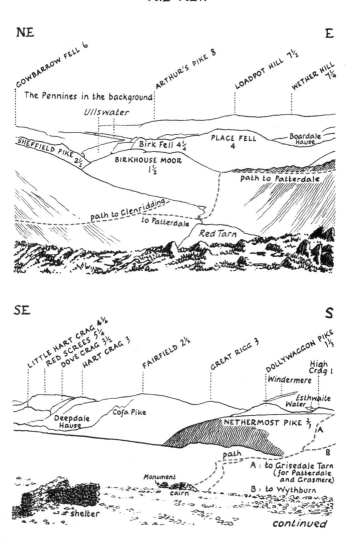

NE   E

COWBARROW FELL 6

The Pennines in the background

ARTHUR'S PIKE 8

LOADPOT HILL 7½

WETHER HILL 7¼

Ullswater

SHEFFIELD PIKE 2½

Birk Fell 4¼

BIRKHOUSE MOOR 1½

PLACE FELL 4

Boardale Hause

path to Patterdale

path to Glenridding

to Patterdale

Red Tarn

SE   S

LITTLE HART CRAG 4¼

RED SCREES 5¼

DOVE CRAG 3½

HART CRAG 3

FAIRFIELD 2½

GREAT RIGG 3

DOLLYWAGGON PIKE 1⅓

High Crag 1

Windermere

Esthwaite Water

Deepdale Hause

Cofa Pike

NETHERMOST PIKE ⅔

A

path

B

Monument

A: to Grisedale Tarn (for Patterdale and Grasmere)

B: to Wythburn

cairn

shelter

continued

THE VIEW

continued

S   SW

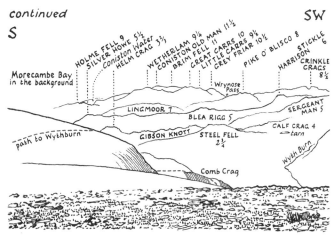

W   NW

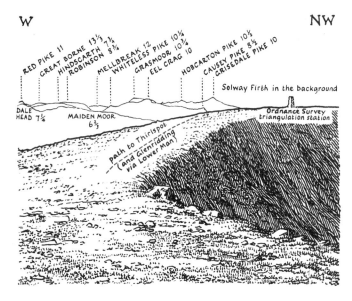

THE VIEW

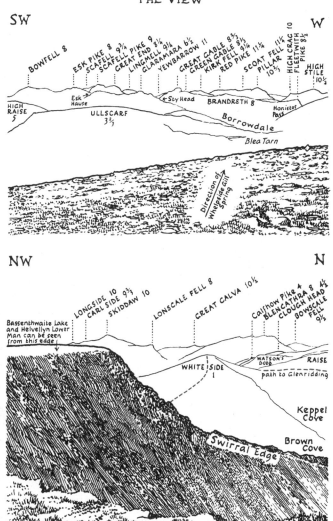

SW   W

BOWFELL 8
ESK PIKE 8
SCAFELL PIKE 9¾
SCAFELL PIKE 9
GREAT END 9¼
LINGMELL 8½
GLARAMARA 6½
YEWBARROW 11
GREAT GABLE 8⅔
GREEN GABLE 8½
KIRK FELL 9½
RED PIKE 11¼
SCOAT FELL 11½
PILLAR 10¾
HIGH CRAG 10
FLEETWITH
PIKE 8½
HIGH STILE 10½

HIGH RAISE 5
Esk Hause
ULLSCARF 3⅔
Sty Head
BRANDRETH 8
Borrowdale
Honister Pass

Blea Tarn

Direction of Whelpside Gill Spring

NW   N

LONGSIDE 10
CARL SIDE 9⅔
SKIDDAW 10
LONSCALE FELL 8
GREAT CALVA 10½
Calfhow Pike 4
BLENCATHRA 8
CLOUGH HEAD 4½
BOWSCALE FELL 9½

Bassenthwaite Lake and Helvellyn Lower Man can be seen from this edge

WHITE SIDE
WATSON'S DODD
RAISE
path to Glenridding

Keppel Cove

Brown Cove

Swirral Edge

Heron Pike

2008'

from Grasmere

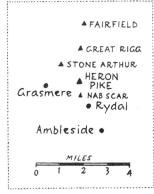

▲ FAIRFIELD

▲ GREAT RIGG

▲ STONE ARTHUR
▲ HERON
    PIKE
Grasmere ● ▲ NAB SCAR
    ● Rydal

Ambleside ●

MILES

0   1   2   3   4

Heron Pike is a grassy mound on the long southern ridge of Fairfield. From no direction does it look like a pike or peak nor will herons be found there. It is a viewpoint of some merit but otherwise is of little interest. It is climbed not, as a rule, for any attraction of its own, but because it happens to lie on a popular route to Fairfield. The ridge beyond it undulates with little change of altitude before rising sharply to Great Rigg, and this hinterland of Heron Pike is generally referred to as Rydal Fell: for convenience it will be described in this chapter as a part of Heron Pike.

NATURAL FEATURES

Heron Pike is the watershed between Rydale and the short Greenhead valley. Grass predominates on its slopes but there is much bracken on the Rydale flank and rock outcrops on both. Its streams are small and flow into the Rothay. A dreary sheet of water named Alcock Tarn, once a reservoir, occupies a shelf above Grasmere; here are many low crags. A nameless summit on the ridge to the north of Heron Pike has a steep east face, which at one point falls away abruptly in a formidable wall of rock, Erne Crag (or Earing Crag), and, further north, the fellside is cleft from top to bottom by a straight stony gully, beyond which the ground becomes rough as Great Rigg is approached. In contrast, the western slopes adjoining Great Rigg are entirely grassy.

Erne Crag

MAP

ONE MILE

continuation GREAT RIGG 3

continuation HART CRAG 3

sheepfold

Greenhead Gill

gully

KESWICK

continuation STONE ARTHUR 2

x ruin

boulder

SWAN Hotel

Erne Crag

AMBLESIDE

Blind Cove

HERON PIKE 2008'

Rydal Beck

N

Alcock Tarn

Lord Crag

GRASMERE

GRASMERE

sheepfold

RYDAL 1

continuation NAB SCAR 2

ASCENTS

Usually the summit of Heron Pike is visited only incidentally on the way to or from Fairfield, but it may be recommended as the objective of an easy and remunerative half-day's walk from Grasmere (using the path from the south end of Alcock Tarn) or from Rydal (climbing Nab Scar *en route*). Gully-addicts will rejoice to learn that a long straight gully, full of shifting scree but with no difficulty other than steepness, falls from the ridge half a mile north of the summit, directly above the sheepfold in mid-Rydale beyond Erne Crag: this offers a scramble they (and they alone) will enjoy, but not even the most avid of them would find any pleasure in *descending* by this route.

THE SUMMIT

The summit is by a little outcrop of rock, distinguished by quartz. All else is grass. There is no cairn and nothing of interest except the view. The nameless north

summit is better: at least it has a wall and a cairn and a few rocks suitable for backrests.
DESCENTS: Any route of ascent (except the gully) may be used for descent. A quick way off to Rydal, in a season when the bracken is short, is by Blind Cove. *In mist*, keep *strictly* to the path going south to Nab Scar and Rydal.

RIDGE ROUTES

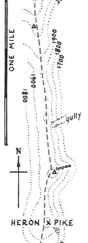

To GREAT RIGG, 2513'
1½ miles : N then NNE
Minor depressions
550 feet of ascent
A pleasant high-level traverse

A good path undulates over grass and finally climbs the cone ahead. Safe in mist.

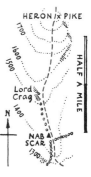

To NAB SCAR, 1450'
⅔ mile : S
Downhill all the way
A very easy descent

The path keeps to the left of the ridge for much of the way, then it follows an old wall. Safe in mist.

THE VIEW

The smallness of the summit gives depth to the views, which are particularly rich in lakes and tarns. Nearby are the fells of the Fairfield Horseshoe, but the best of the mountain scene is formed by the finely-grouped Coniston and Langdale fells with Scafell Pike overtopping all.

Principal Fells

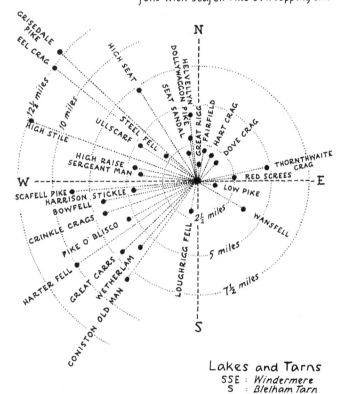

Lakes and Tarns

SSE : *Windermere*
S : *Blelham Tarn*
S : *Wise Een Tarn*
S : *Esthwaite Water*
SSW : *Coniston Water*
SSW : *Elterwater*
W : *Easedale Tarn*

High Hartsop Dodd

1702'

from Dovedale Beck

Patterdale

Hartsop

Hartsop
Hall
DOVE CRAG ▲ HIGH
HARTSOP
LITTLE ▲ DODD
HART CRAG

RED ▲ SCREES
MILES
0   1   2   3

High Hartsop Dodd, seen from the valley near Brothers Water, has the appearance of an isolated mountain with a peaked summit and steep sides, a very shapely pyramid rising from green fields. But in fact it is merely the termination of a spur of a higher fell, Little Hart Crag, which it partly hides from view, and its uninteresting grassy summit has little distinction, though it is always greeted with enthusiasm by walkers who attain it direct from the valley, for the upper slopes above the sparsely-wooded lower flanks are excessively steep. A high ascending ridge links the Dodd with the rough top of Little Hart Crag.

MAP

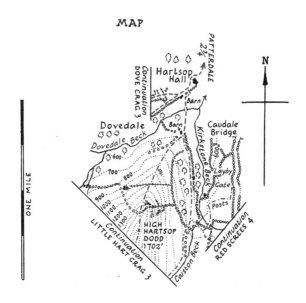

ASCENT FROM HARTSOP HALL
1200 feet of ascent

High Hartsop Dodd may be climbed direct from the barn at its foot — note here the symmetry between the pitch of the roof of the barn as it is approached across the boulder-dotted pastures from Hartsop Hall, and the sides of the pyramid of the Dodd behind — but the steepness of the grass slope, especially as the top wall is neared, makes the ascent laborious. It is really much better first to ascend Little Hart Crag (preferably by way of Dovedale) and to return to the valley over the top of the Dodd.

High Hartsop Dodd can also be ascended from the layby to the south of Caudale Bridge.

THE SUMMIT

There is no cairn to indicate the highest point – all is grass – and indeed it is not easy to say which is the summit; but it is assumed to be the top of the *first* rise above the broken wall. *In descending, in mist,* remember that the wall does not cross the ridge at right-angles, but at a tangent Do NOT follow the wall down: on both flanks it leads to crags.

> This unassuming fell had its brief period of glory in 1948 when it won headlines in the newspapers by the efforts of rescuers to save two terriers trapped in a hole on the steep Caiston flank.

Dove Crag and Hogget Gill, from High Hartsop Dodd

THE VIEW

The most striking feature in a moderate view is the exceptionally fine picture of Dovedale, which is seen intimately in all its strong and impressive contrasts.

Lakes and Tarns
NNE: *Brothers Water*

Principal Fells

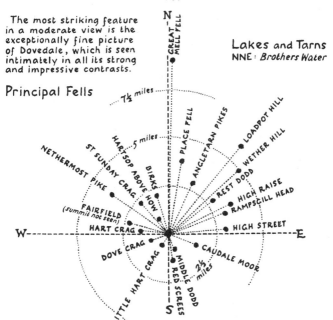

Brothers Water

High Pike

2155'

sometimes referred to as
Scandale Fell

from High Sweden Bridge

▲ DOVE CRAG

▲ HIGH PIKE

▲ LOW PIKE

• Rydal

• Ambleside

MILES
0   1   2   3

Everest enthusiasts will likken the two pronounced rises on the long southern spur of Dove Crag to the 'first and second steps' on the famous north-east ridge (but imagination would indeed have to be vivid to see in the grassy dome of Dove Crag any resemblance to the icy pyramid of that highest of all peaks!). The first rise is Low Pike, the second is High Pike. The latter, with its cairn perched on the brink of a shattered cliff, is the most imposing object seen from Scandale which lies far below.

Some authorities refer to High Pike as Scandale Fell, but the latter name is more properly applied in a general way to the whole of the high ground enclosing Scandale Bottom to north and west.

NATURAL FEATURES

Viewed from the south, High Pike has the appearance of an isolated peak; viewed from the parallel ridges to east and west, it is seen in its true proportions as merely the flat top of a rise in Dove Crag's long southern ridge; viewed from the north, it is entirely insignificant. High Pike, therefore, cannot be regarded as having enough qualifications to make it a mountain in its own right. Its level top, however, marks a definite change in the character of the ridge, which is narrow and rocky below and broad and grassy above. The western flank of High Pike descends to Rydale in uninteresting slopes relieved by occasional outcrops of rock; the eastern face is much rougher and steeper, with an ill-defined stony shoulder going down into Scandale.

MAP

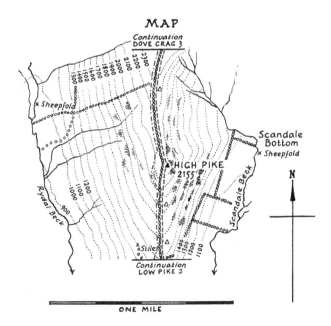

NOTE: On Bartholomews 1" Map the summit is shown as 'Scandale Fell.'

ASCENT FROM AMBLESIDE
2000 feet of ascent : 4 miles

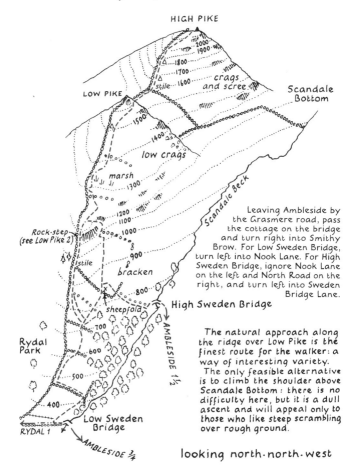

HIGH PIKE

2000
1900
1800
1700
crags
and scree
stile 1600
LOW PIKE
Scandale Bottom
1500

1400
low crags

marsh
1300

Scandale Beck

1200
1100
1000
Rock-step
(see Low Pike 2)
stile
900
bracken
800

sheepfold
High Sweden Bridge

700
Rydal Park
AMBLESIDE 1½
600

500

400
Low Sweden Bridge

RYDAL 1
AMBLESIDE ¾

Leaving Ambleside by the Grasmere road, pass the cottage on the bridge and turn right into Smithy Brow. For Low Sweden Bridge, turn left into Nook Lane. For High Sweden Bridge, ignore Nook Lane on the left and North Road on the right, and turn left into Sweden Bridge Lane.

The natural approach along the ridge over Low Pike is the finest route for the walker: a way of interesting variety. The only feasible alternative is to climb the shoulder above Scandale Bottom: there is no difficulty here, but it is a dull ascent and will appeal only to those who like steep scrambling over rough ground.

looking north·north·west

This route, commonly used as the initial stage of the 'Fairfield Horseshoe', provides a pleasant walk along a good ridge. The lower approaches are very attractive.

THE SUMMIT

The summit is a flat grassy promenade with a cairn standing at the northern end on the edge of a decaying crag, overlooking Scandale. A high wall runs along the top.

DESCENTS: The ridge-path should always be used when leaving the top: nothing but discomfort is to be gained by attempting a direct descent to east or west.

In bad weather conditions, a safe descent may be made to Ambleside by following the ridge over Low Pike, keeping to the path, or, if the path is lost, to the wall.   A journey to Patterdale need not be abandoned in the event of bad weather on High Pike: the safe conclusion of the walk is ensured if the wall is followed north to a broken fence, which leads down grassy slopes to Dovedale or, alternatively, to Scandale Pass.

The wall

A traveller along the ridge cannot help but notice the wall: it accompanies him all the way and its intimacy becomes a nuisance. However, it is well worthy of notice, particularly on the steepest rises south of the summit, where the method and style of construction, in persevering horizontal courses despite the difficulties of the ground, compel admiration: it should be remembered, too, that all the stone had to be found on the fell and cut to shape on the site. Witness here a dying art!

RIDGE ROUTES

To DOVE CRAG, 2598' : 1 mile : N.
Slight depression : 470 feet of ascent
An easy, gradual climb on grass. Perfectly safe in mist.

Follow the wall north; an intermittent path keeps a few yards to the right of it. The cairn does not come into sight until a broken fence is reached.

To LOW PIKE, 1667' : ⅔ mile : S.
Depression at 1575'
100 feet of ascent
An easy walk downhill on a rough but distinct path. Safe in mist.

The path keeps to the left of the wall and skirts the base of the top pyramid of Low Pike, the summit being attained by a short steep scramble.

from Scandale

THE VIEW

The ridge-wall obstructs the view westwards from the cairn but is worth surmounting for the prospect of the Central Fells, which is good. In other directions, neighbouring higher fells hide the distance, but much of the High Street range is seen over the Scandale Pass.

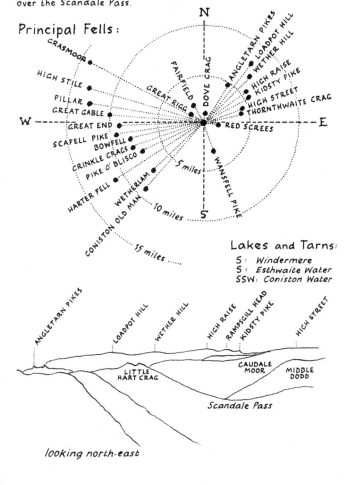

Principal Fells:

N

CRASMOOR

HIGH STILE

PILLAR

GREAT GABLE

GREAT END

SCAFELL PIKE

BOWFELL

CRINKLE CRAGS

PIKE O' BLISCO

HARTER FELL

WETHERLAM

CONISTON OLD MAN

FAIRFIELD

GREAT RIGG

DOVE CRAG

ANGLETARN PIKES

LOADPOT HILL

WETHER HILL

HIGH RAISE

KIDSTY PIKE

HIGH STREET

THORNTHWAITE CRAG

RED SCREES

WANSFELL PIKE

W — — — E

5 miles

10 miles

15 miles ....

S

Lakes and Tarns:

S: *Windermere*
S: *Esthwaite Water*
SSW: *Coniston Water*

ANGLETARN PIKES

LOADPOT HILL

WETHER HILL

HIGH RAISE

RAMPSGILL HEAD

KIDSTY PIKE

HIGH STREET

LITTLE HART CRAG

CAUDALE MOOR

MIDDLE DODD

Scandale Pass

looking north-east

Little Hart Crag 2091'

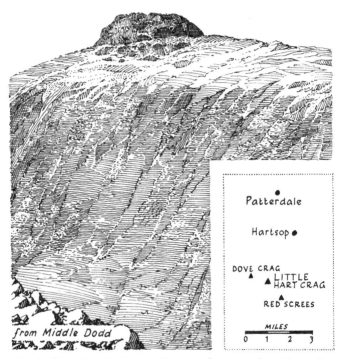

Patterdale

Hartsop •

DOVE CRAG
▲   ▲ LITTLE
      HART CRAG

▲ RED SCREES

MILES
0   1   2   3

from Middle Dodd

Little Hart Crag is the sentinel of Scandale Pass, four miles north of Ambleside, and takes its duty of guarding the Pass very seriously and proudly. It has the appearance, in fact, of a crouching watchdog, facing Scandale and missing nothing of the happenings there, while its spine curves down to the fields of Hartsop; the path from one place to the other climbs over its shoulder just beneath the hoary head and beetling brows.

It is really a very junior member in a company of grand hills and quite overshadowed by Red Screes and Dove Crag; but it has individuality and an interesting double summit which commands delightful views of Scandale and Dovedale.

NATURAL FEATURES

Little Hart Crag descends in uninteresting slopes of grass and bracken to Scandale in the south; it is connected in the west to Dove Crag by the broad marshy depression of Bakestones Moss; south-east is the lower depression of Scandale Pass and the vast soaring flank of Red Screes. North-east is a narrow spur running at a high elevation before plunging sharply to the valley at Hartsop: this

The summit, from the south

is High Hartsop Dodd, and its steep-sided pyramidal form, seen from Brothers Water, gives it the appearance of being a separate height. Just below the summit, west, is a long wall of impressive crags, Black Brow. The eastern slopes, falling to Caiston Glen, are rough and unattractive.

Hartsop, from the summit

MAP

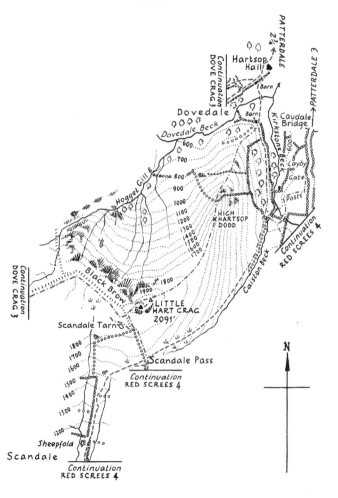

ONE MILE

ASCENT FROM PATTERDALE
1,700 feet of ascent : 5 miles from Patterdale village

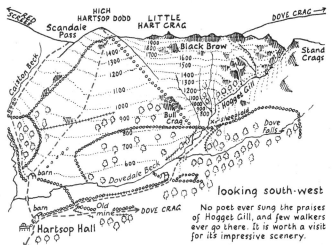

looking south-west

No poet ever sung the praises of Hogget Gill, and few walkers ever go there. It is worth a visit for its impressive scenery.

The easiest route is by Caiston Glen, turning right at Scandale Pass; the most interesting is via Hogget Gill, *which must not be attempted in mist.* The direct route over High Hartsop Dodd is steep.

ASCENT FROM AMBLESIDE
2,000 feet of ascent : 4¼ miles

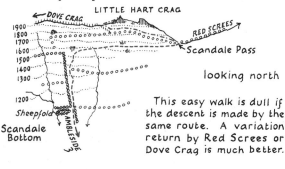

looking north

This easy walk is dull if the descent is made by the same route. A variation return by Red Screes or Dove Crag is much better.

THE SUMMIT

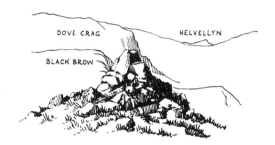

DOVE CRAG

HELVELLYN

BLACK BROW

There are two well-defined tops. The higher is that nearer to Dove Crag; it is surmounted by a cairn perched on the extreme edge of a rocky platform. The lower summit, to the north-east, is less conspicuous, but is easily identified in mist by markings of quartz in the stones near the insignificant cairn: this cairn is the key to the ridge going down to High Hartsop Dodd. Both summits are buttressed to the south by sheer walls of black rock.

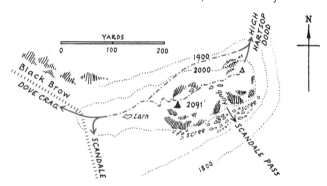

DESCENTS: The descent to Patterdale is best made directly by the grassy ridge over High Hartsop Dodd, the last 1000 feet down to the valley being steep. Scandale, for Ambleside, may be reached by cutting off a corner at the top of the pass.
In mist, the summit is confusing and dangerous. The safest way off is west to the broken fence, following this down south to Scandale Pass for either Patterdale or Ambleside. Descents to Caiston Glen or Dovedale direct should not be attempted.

THE VIEW

Principal Fells

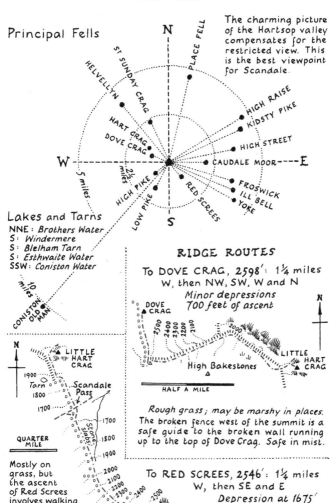

The charming picture of the Hartsop valley compensates for the restricted view. This is the best viewpoint for Scandale.

N

ST SUNDAY CRAG
HELVELLYN
PLACE FELL
HART CRAG
DOVE CRAG
HIGH RAISE
KIDSTY PIKE
HIGH STREET
W — CAUDALE MOOR ----E
5 miles
2½ miles
HIGH PIKE
LOW PIKE
RED SCREES
FROSWICK
ILL BELL
YOKE
S

Lakes and Tarns
NNE: Brothers Water
S: Windermere
S: Blelham Tarn
S: Esthwaite Water
SSW: Coniston Water

10 miles
CONISTON OLD MAN

N
LITTLE HART CRAG
1900
Tarn
1800
Scandale Pass
1700
1700
Stone Slabs
1800
QUARTER MILE
1900

Mostly on grass, but the ascent of Red Screes involves walking along sloping slabs of rock.

RIDGE ROUTES

TO DOVE CRAG, 2598′: 1¼ miles
W, then NW, SW, W and N
Minor depressions
700 feet of ascent

N

DOVE CRAG
2500 2400 2300 2200 2100 2000
LITTLE HART CRAG
High Bakestones

HALF A MILE

Rough grass; may be marshy in places. The broken fence west of the summit is a safe guide to the broken wall running up to the top of Dove Crag. Safe in mist.

TO RED SCREES, 2546′: 1¼ miles
W, then SE and E
Depression at 1675′
900 feet of ascent
An easy and tedious walk.

2000 2100 2200 2300 2400 2500
RED SCREES

Little Mell Fell

from Gowbarrow Fell

Little Mell Fell barely merits inclusion in this book. It *is* a fell — its name says so — but it is not the stuff of which the true fells are made. It rises on the verge of Lakeland but its characteristics are alien to Lakeland. It stands in isolation, not in the company of others. Its substance looks more akin to the sandstones of the nearby valley of Eden; its patchwork clothing, gorse and ling prominent, is unusual on the other fells; its hedges of stunted, windblown, unhappy trees and tumbledown fences are unsatisfactory substitutes for friendly stone walls. It is ringed by a quiet and pleasant countryside of green pastures and lush hedgerows, and one is as likely to meet a cow as a sheep on its slopes. There is good in all, however, and its heathery top is a fine place for viewing the (greater) merits of other fells.

• Penruddock

GREAT MELL FELL
▲

Pooley
Bridge •

LITTLE ▲
MELL FELL

Watermillock
▲ GOWBARROW FELL

• Dockray

MILES
0   1   2   3   4

NATURAL FEATURES

Little Mell Fell is an outlier of the Helvellyn range and the last Lakeland fell in the north-east before the high country falls away to the wide plain stretching to the distant Border. It is an uninspiring, unattractive, bare and rounded hump — the sublime touch that made a wonderland of the district overlooked Little Mell — and few walkers halt their hurried entrance into the sanctuary to climb and explore it. In truth, there is little to explore. As though conscious of its failings it tries to aspire to normal mountain structure by throwing out two ridges, but the effort is weak and not convincing. One feels sorry for Little Mell Fell, as for all who are neglected and forlorn, but at least it is beloved of birds and animals and it is one of the few fells that grouse select for their habitat, and not even the great Helvellyn itself can make such a claim!

MAP

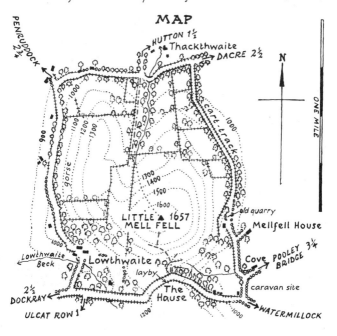

ASCENTS

The fell is almost entirely enclosed within fences and hedges but access may be gained from the Hause and from the bridge near Thackthwaite.

It is difficult to plan a mountaineering expedition within a single square mile of territory, and probably it is best to climb straight up and down from the Hause and get the job done without frills: half an hour is sufficient from here. An alternative approach lies along the wooded hollow above the charming bridge near Thackthwaite and makes use of an old droveway with ditches on either side. Walkers using this route are encouraged by two stiles near the start, but after struggling in the mud for half a mile they are confronted by a barbed wire fence without a stile, and by this time they will be wishing that they had approached the fell from the Hause.

THE SUMMIT

On the highest point is an Ordnance Survey column. The stone wall that formerly stood nearby has gone, and so has all the heather that once covered the top. The town of Penrith is well seen from the summit, with the village of Dacre directly below.

DESCENTS: Descents may safely be made in any direction, in any weather, without the remotest risk of accident by falling over a crag; frisky bullocks are the only obstacles to be feared. The Hause, to which descents will be made usually, is not visible from the summit but comes into sight below by walking south, in the direction of Hallin Fell: beware rabbit-holes obscured by bracken on this slope.

Great Mell Fell from Little Mell Fell

THE VIEW

The diagram illustrates effectively the isolated situation of Little Mell Fell on the fringe of mountain country. One half of the view is of Lakeland, the other half of lowlands stretching away to the Pennines and the Border across the lovely Vale of Eden.
This is one of the few good viewpoints for appreciating the shy beauty of Martindale.
Gowbarrow Fell hides most of Ullswater, only the unexciting lower reach of the lake being in sight.

Principal Fells

Lakes and Tarns
SE : *Ullswater*

Low Pike

1667'

from Rydal Beck

▲ HIGH PIKE

▲ LOW PIKE

● Rydal

● Ambleside

MILES

0 1 2 3

Low Pike is well seen from the streets of Ambleside as the first prominent peak on the high ridge running northwards. The gradient along the crest of the ridge is slight, but Low Pike, halfway along, is sufficiently elevated above the deep valleys of Scandale, east, and Rydale, west, to give an impression of loftiness which exaggerates its modest altitude. There is a good deal of rock on the fell with several tiers of low crag. Low Pike is the objective in the fell-races at the annual sports meetings in Rydal Park.

MAP

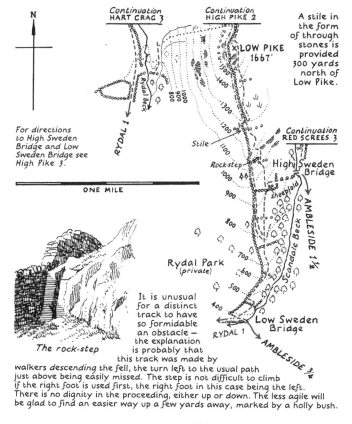

N

Continuation
HART CRAG 3

Continuation
HIGH PIKE 2

×LOW PIKE
1667'

A stile in
the form
of through
stones is
provided
300 yards
north of
Low Pike.

Rydal Beck

RYDAL 1

For directions
to High Sweden
Bridge and Low
Sweden Bridge see
High Pike 3.

ONE MILE

Stile

Continuation
RED SCREES 3

Rock-step

High Sweden
Bridge

sheepfold

AMBLESIDE 1½

Scandale Beck

Rydal Park
(private)

Low Sweden
Bridge

RYDAL 1

AMBLESIDE ¾

The rock-step

It is unusual
for a distinct
track to have
so formidable
an obstacle —
the explanation
is probably that
this track was made by
walkers descending the fell, the turn left to the usual path
just above being easily missed. The step is not difficult to climb
if the right foot is used first, the right foot in this case being the left.
There is no dignity in the proceeding, either up or down. The less agile will
be glad to find an easier way up a few yards away, marked by a holly bush.

ASCENTS

Low Pike is invariably climbed from Ambleside, usually on
the way to the high fells beyond; it is, however, an excellent
objective for a short walk from that town. The approach, by
any of the variations, from the pleasant woods and pastures
to the bleak craggy ridge is very attractive. The wall along
the watershed detracts from the merits of this enjoyable walk.
  The climb from Rydal Beck is tedious; there is no path. Aged
pedestrians should note two hazards on this route: the crossing
of the beck first, and the scaling of the ridge-wall finally.

THE SUMMIT

High Pike

The summit is an abrupt rocky peak, a place of grey boulders and small grassy platforms in the shadow of a substantial stone wall. Some of the rocks near the summit are big enough to afford simple practice in climbing. There is no cairn nor room for one: the wall occupies the highest inches.

DESCENTS: The way to Ambleside would be obvious even if there was no path. The point of divergence at 1200' is not clear: if the wall is followed beware the rock-step, which appears unexpectedly. For Rydal, follow the wall south and turn right at Low Sweden Bridge (*see Dove Crag 5*).

In mist, all descents should be made to Ambleside, keeping strictly to the path, or, if the path be lost, to the wall. There are crags at the 1200' level.

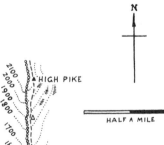

Step-stile

Highest point

1400
1500

Large cairn

YARDS

300
200
100
0

AMBLESIDE

N

HALF A MILE

2100
2000
1900
1800
1700
1600
1500

▲ HIGH PIKE

Step-stile

LOW PIKE

RIDGE ROUTE

To HIGH PIKE, 2155': ⅔ mile : N.
Depression at 1575': 600 feet of ascent.
  A straightforward walk, safe in mist.
A distinct path follows the wall, climbing steadily most of the way amongst rocks.

THE VIEW

All the attractiveness of the scene is centred between south and west, where the Coniston and Langdale fells rise grandly from a lowland of lakes.

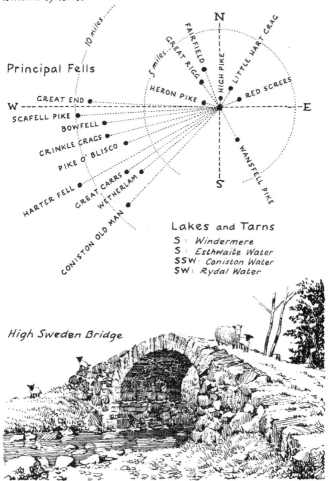

Principal Fells

10 miles

5 miles

N

FAIRFIELD
GREAT RIGG
HERON PIKE
HIGH PIKE
LITTLE HART CRAG
RED SCREES

W — GREAT END
SCAFELL PIKE
BOWFELL
CRINKLE CRAGS
PIKE O' BLISCO
HARTER FELL
GREAT CARRS
WETHERLAM
CONISTON OLD MAN

— E

WANSFELL PIKE

S

Lakes and Tarns

S : Windermere
S : Esthwaite Water
SSW : Coniston Water
SW : Rydal Water

High Sweden Bridge

Middle Dodd
2146'

from Caiston Glen

Patterdale

Hartsop

Hartsop
Hall

DOVE CRAG
▲ MIDDLE DODD
▲

RED ▲ SCREES

MILES

0   1   2   3

To the traveller starting the long climb
up to Kirkstone Pass from Brothers Water
the most striking object in a fine array
of mountain scenery is the steep pyramid
ahead: it towers high above the road like
a gigantic upturned boat, its keel touching
the sky, its sides barnacled and hoary.
This pyramid is Middle Dodd, the middle
one of three dodds which rise from the
pastures of Hartsop, all exhibiting the
same characteristics. When seen from
higher ground in the vicinity, however,
Middle Dodd loses its regal appearance
(as do the other two); its summit then
is obviously nothing more than a halt in
the long northern spur of Red Screes.

MAP

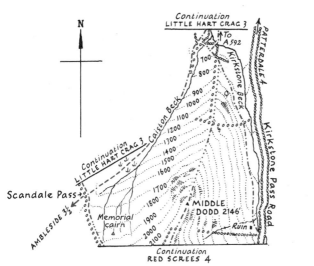

Continuation
LITTLE HART CRAG 3

To
A 592

N

Kirkstone Beck

PATTERDALE 4

Kirkstone Pass Road

700
800
900
1000
1100
1200
1300
1400
1500
1600
1700
1800
1900
2000
2100

Continuation
LITTLE HART CRAG 3

Caiston Beck

Scandale Pass

AMBLESIDE 3½

Memorial cairn

▲ MIDDLE DODD 2146

Ruin

ONE MILE

Continuation
RED SCREES 4

ASCENT FROM HARTSOP HALL
1650 feet of ascent

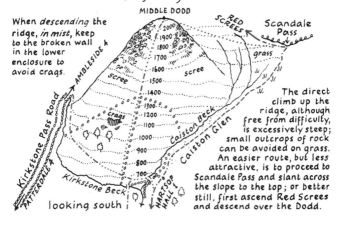

MIDDLE DODD

RED SCREES

Scandale Pass

When *descending* the ridge, *in mist*, keep to the broken wall in the lower enclosure to avoid crags.

AMBLESIDE

Kirkstone Pass Road

PATTERDALE

scree

2000
1900
1800
1700
1600
1500
1400
1300
1200
1100
1000
900
800
700

crags

scree

grass

Caiston Beck

Caiston Glen

Kirkstone Beck

HARTSOP HALL

looking south

The direct climb up the ridge, although free from difficulty, is excessively steep; small outcrops of rock can be avoided on grass. An easier route, but less attractive, is to proceed to Scandale Pass and slant across the slope to the top; or better still, first ascend Red Screes and descend over the Dodd.

THE SUMMIT

The top of Middle Dodd is a rather narrow grassy promenade. The ground immediately behind the rocky promontory which serves as the triangulation point rises gently to a knoll some forty feet higher — here is the summit-cairn — before falling imperceptibly to the saddle linking Middle Dodd to Red Screes.

Near the cairn is a series of curious depressions like a line of sinkholes in limestone country, but as the rock here is volcanic the probability is that they are old earthworks; the detached boulders strewn about in them seem to suggest artificial excavation. Walkers who are neither archæologists nor geologists will see in the depressions only a refuge from the wind.

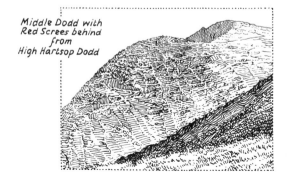

Middle Dodd with
Red Screes behind
from
High Hartsop Dodd

THE VIEW

Considering that Middle Dodd is hemmed in on all sides by higher fells, the view is remarkably good, and unexpectedly extensive in the south-west.

Principal Fells

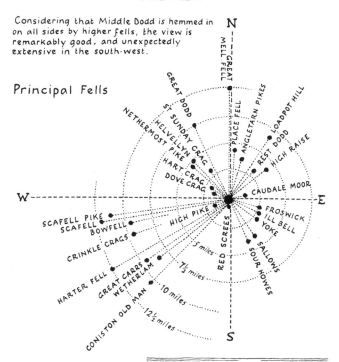

Principal fells panorama with radial bearings

Fells labelled (clockwise from north): GREAT MELL FELL, GREAT DODD, St SUNDAY CRAG, HELVELLYN, NETHERMOST PIKE, HART CRAG, DOVE CRAG, PLACE FELL, ANGLETARN PIKES, LOADPOT HILL, REST DODD, HIGH RAISE, CAUDALE MOOR, FROSWICK, ILL BELL, YOKE, SALLOWS, SOUR HOWES, RED SCREES, HIGH PIKE, SCAFELL PIKE, SCAFELL, BOWFELL, CRINKLE CRAGS, HARTER FELL, GREAT CARRS, WETHERLAM, CONISTON OLD MAN

Distance rings: 5 miles, 7½ miles, 10 miles, 12½ miles

Lakes and Tarns

N : *Ullswater*
N : *Brothers Water*
SW: *Greenburn Tarn*
       (below Great Carrs)

looking north

Nab Scar

1450'

▲ FAIRFIELD

▲ GREAT RIGG

▲ STONE ARTHUR

▲ HERON PIKE

Grasmere ▲ NAB SCAR
• Rydal

Ambleside •

MILES

0 1 2 3 4

from Rydal Water

NATURAL FEATURES

Nab Scar is well known. Its associations with the Lake Poets who came to dwell at the foot of its steep wooded slopes have invested it with romance, and its commanding position overlooking Rydal Water brings it to the notice of the many visitors to that charming lake. It is a fine abrupt height, with a rough, craggy south face; on the flanks are easier slopes. Elevated ground continues beyond the summit and rises gently to Heron Pike. Nab Scar is not a separate fell, but is merely the butt of the long southern ridge of Fairfield.

MAP

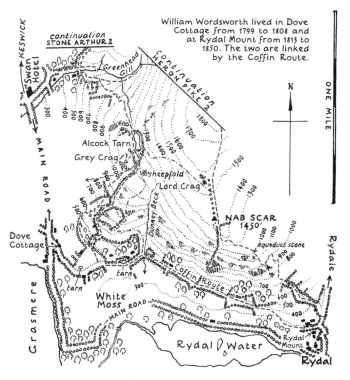

William Wordsworth lived in Dove Cottage from 1799 to 1808 and at Rydal Mount from 1813 to 1850. The two are linked by the Coffin Route.

ASCENTS

The popular ascent is from Rydal, a charming climb along a good path, steep in its middle reaches; this is the beginning of the 'Fairfield Horseshoe' when it is walked clockwise. Nab Scar can also be reached from the Swan Hotel by means of a path that rises from the south end of Alcock Tarn.

THE SUMMIT

Strictly, Nab Scar is the name of the craggy south face, not of the fell rising above it, but its recognised summit is a tall edifice of stones built well back from the edge of the cliffs, near a crumbled wall that runs north towards Heron Pike. Hereabouts the immediate surroundings are uninteresting, the redeeming feature being the fine view.

Nab Scar has a subterranean watercourse: below its surface the Thirlmere aqueduct runs through a tunnel. The scars of this operation are nearly gone, but evidence of the existence of the tunnel remains alongside the Rydal path, above the steepest part: here may be found a block of stone a yard square set in the ground; it bears no inscription but marks the position of the tunnel directly beneath.

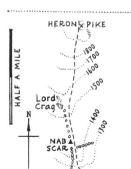

RIDGE ROUTE

To HERON PIKE, 2008': ⅔ mile: N
570 feet of ascent
An easy climb on grass
A plain path accompanies the old wall, then it keeps to the right of the ridge.

THE VIEW

This is an 'unbalanced' view, most of it being exceptionally dull, the rest exceptionally charming. Lakes and tarns are a very special feature of the delightful prospect to south and west and the grouping of the Coniston and Langdale fells is quite attractive.

Principal Fells

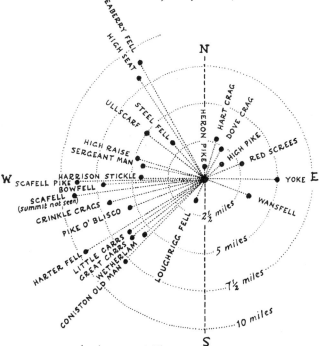

Lakes and Tarns

SSE : *Windermere*
S : *Blelham Tarn*
S : *Esthwaite Water*
SSW : *Coniston Water*
SW : *Elterwater*
WSW : *Grasmere*
WNW : *Easedale Tarn*
NW : *Alcock Tarn*

Nethermost Pike   2920′

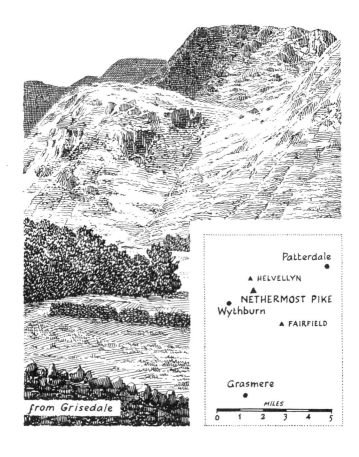

from Grisedale

Patterdale •

▲ HELVELLYN
▲
• NETHERMOST PIKE
Wythburn
▲ FAIRFIELD

Grasmere
•

MILES
0 1 2 3 4 5

NATURAL FEATURES

Thousands of people cross the flat top of Nethermost Pike every year, and thousands more toil up its western slope. Yet their diaries record "climbed Helvellyn today." For Helvellyn is the great magnet that draws the crowds to Nethermost Pike: the latter is climbed incidentally, almost unknowingly, only because it is an obstacle in the route to its bigger neighbour. The grassy west slope trodden by the multitudes is of little interest, but the fell should not be judged accordingly: it is made of sterner stuff. From the east, Nethermost Pike is magnificent, hardly less so than Helvellyn and seeming more so because of its impressive surroundings. On this side a narrow rocky ridge bounded by forbidding crags falls steeply between twin hollows, deeply recessed, in a wild and lonely setting; here is solitude, for here few men walk. Here, too, is a gem of a tarn.

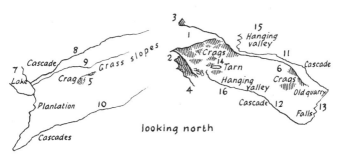

looking north

1 The summit of Nethermost Pike
2 High Crag
3 Ridge continuing to Helvellyn
4 Ridge continuing to Dollywaggon Pike
5 Comb Crag
6 Eagle Crag
7 Thirlmere
8 Whelpside Gill
9 Comb Gill
10 Birkside Gill
11 Nethermostcove Beck
12 Ruthwaite Beck
13 Grisedale Beck
14 Hard Tarn
15 Nethermost Cove
16 Ruthwaite Cove

The North Face

MAP

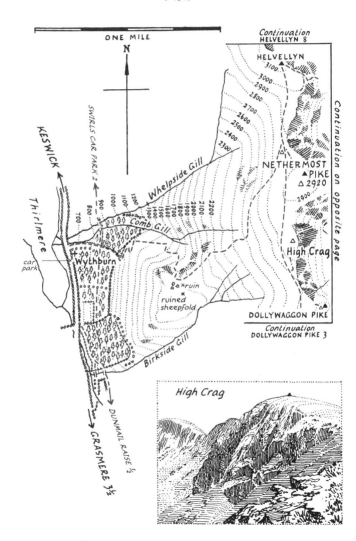

ONE MILE

N

Continuation
HELVELLYN 8

HELVELLYN

3100
3000
2900
2800
2700
2600
2500
2400
2300

KESWICK

Thirlmere

SWIRLS CAR PARK 2

Whelpside Gill

Comb Gill

900
1000
1100
1200
800
700
1300
1400
1500
1600
1700
1800
1900
2000
2100
2200

NETHERMOST
PIKE
2920

2900

car park

Wythburn

ruin
×
ruined sheepfold

High Crag

DOLLYWAGGON PIKE

Continuation
DOLLYWAGGON PIKE 3

Continuation on opposite page

Birkside Gill

DUNMAIL RAISE ½

GRASMERE 3½

High Crag

MAP

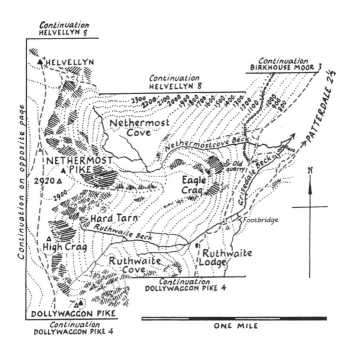

Continuation
HELVELLYN 8

▲ HELVELLYN

Continuation
BIRKHOUSE MOOR 3

Continuation
HELVELLYN 8

PATTERDALE 2½

Continuation on opposite page

Nethermost
Cove

NETHERMOST
PIKE ▲

2920 △

2900

Nethermostcove Beck

Old
quarry

Eagle
Crag

Grisedale Beck

N

Hard Tarn

Ruthwaite Beck

Footbridge

High Crag △

Ruthwaite
Cove

Ruthwaite
Lodge

Continuation
DOLLYWAGGON PIKE 4

△△ DOLLYWAGGON PIKE

Continuation
DOLLYWAGGON PIKE 4

ONE MILE

Hard Tarn

ASCENT FROM WYTHBURN
2400 feet of ascent : 2 miles

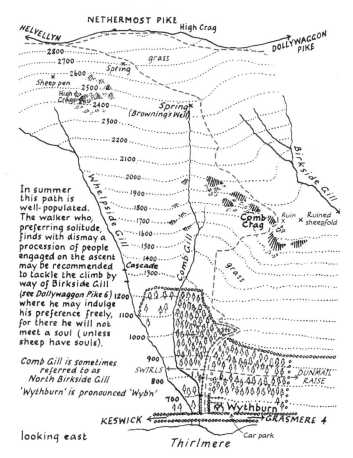

NETHERMOST PIKE

HELVELLYN

High Crag

DOLLYWAGGON PIKE

2800
2700
2600
Spring
grass
2500
Sheep pen
High
Crags
2400
Spring
(Browning's Well)
2300
2200
2100
2000
1900
1800
Comb
Crag
1700
Ruin
Ruined
sheepfold
1600
1500
1400
Cascade
1300
1200
1100
1000
900
SWIRLS
DUNMAIL
RAISE
800
700
Wythburn
KESWICK
GRASMERE 4
Car park
Thirlmere

Whelpside Gill

Comb Gill

Birkside Gill

grass

In summer
this path is
well-populated.
The walker who,
preferring solitude,
finds with dismay a
procession of people
engaged on the ascent
may be recommended
to tackle the climb by
way of Birkside Gill
(see Dollywaggon Pike 6)
where he may indulge
his preference freely,
for there he will not
meet a soul (unless
sheep have souls).

Comb Gill is sometimes
referred to as
North Birkside Gill

'Wythburn' is pronounced 'Wyb'n'

looking east

The popular path to Helvellyn from Wythburn climbs
steeply up the side of Nethermost Pike, almost reaching
its summit before turning off to the higher fell: the top
is attained by a short detour. The path is very distinct.

ASCENT FROM GRISEDALE
2500 feet of ascent : 5 miles from Patterdale village

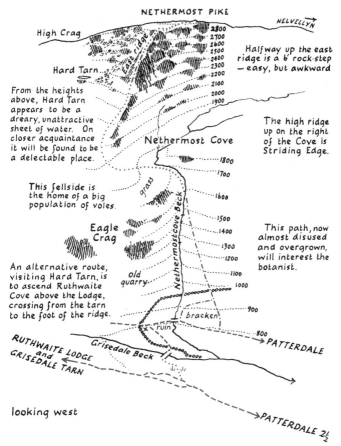

NETHERMOST PIKE

HELVELLYN →

High Crag

2800
2700
2600
2500
2400
2300
2200
2100
2000
1900

East ridge

Hard Tarn

Halfway up the east ridge is a 6' rock-step — easy, but awkward

From the heights above, Hard Tarn appears to be a dreary, unattractive sheet of water. On closer acquaintance it will be found to be a delectable place.

Nethermost Cove

1800
1700

The high ridge up on the right of the Cove is Striding Edge.

grass

1600

This fellside is the home of a big population of voles.

Eagle Crag

1500
1400
1300
1200

Nethermostcove Beck

This path, now almost disused and overgrown, will interest the botanist.

An alternative route, visiting Hard Tarn, is to ascend Ruthwaite Cove above the Lodge, crossing from the tarn to the foot of the ridge.

old quarry

1100
1000

900

bracken

ruin

800

PATTERDALE →

RUTHWAITE LODGE and GRISEDALE TARN

Grisedale Beck

PATTERDALE 2½ →

looking west

This is a first-class route for scramblers, but staid walkers should avoid it and proceed via Grisedale Tarn. The east ridge is steep and exciting, finishing with an arête like a miniature Striding Edge. *This route should not be attempted in bad weather conditions.*

THE SUMMIT

The summit is of considerable extent and so remarkably flat that it is not easy to understand why the name 'Pike' was given to the fell (the top of the east ridge, however, has the appearance of a peak when seen from mid-Grisedale). It is mainly grassy — a field on top of a mountain — with thin flakes of rock around the cairn.

The broad top is level, and it is difficult to locate the highest point exactly, but the cairn illustrated appears to be slightly higher than the small crescent-shaped windshelter, facing west, which lies approximately 100 yards to the southwest.

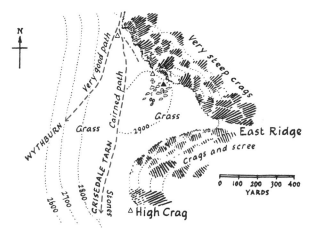

DESCENTS : A cairned path crosses the top but does not visit the actual summit. This path may be followed south to Grisedale Tarn for Grasmere or Patterdale. For Wythburn, cross this path to another running lower along the fellside. The east ridge is a quick way down to Patterdale, but is for experienced walkers only. *In bad weather conditions,* leave the summit by one of the two paths mentioned : these are quite safe — *the east ridge is not.*

RIDGE ROUTES

To HELVELLYN, 3118': ¾ mile : NW then N.

Depression at 2840' : 280 feet of ascent

An easy walk on a broad path, safe in mist.

The path west of the cairn on Nethermost Pike continues north to Helvellyn, developing into a wide uninteresting highway. It is far better, in clear weather, to avoid the path and follow the edge of the cliffs, the views of Nethermost Cove and Striding Edge being very impressive.

To DOLLYWAGGON PIKE, 2815'
1 mile : S then SE

Depression at 2700': 120 feet of ascent

A very easy walk, safe in mist

The path west of the cairn on Nethermost Pike continues south, skirting High Crag. It crosses the breast of Dollywaggon Pike, the summit of which is gained by a short detour. (An inexperienced walker should not attempt the detour in mist). A more interesting route, in clear weather, is to follow the edge of the cliffs overlooking Hard Tarn and Ruthwaite Cove, the rock-scenery being impressive.

Cascades in Birkside Gill

THE VIEW

Northwards, nearby Helvellyn shuts out the distant view, but in all other directions the panorama is very extensive. Nevertheless, the cairn is not a satisfactory viewpoint because the wide expanse of the summit-plateau occupies too much of the picture. A much more attractive and better-balanced view is obtained from the big cairn on High Crag to the south: from here the mountain scene is more pleasing, and additional lakes are visible, i.e. Bassenthwaite Lake, Coniston Water, Esthwaite Water.

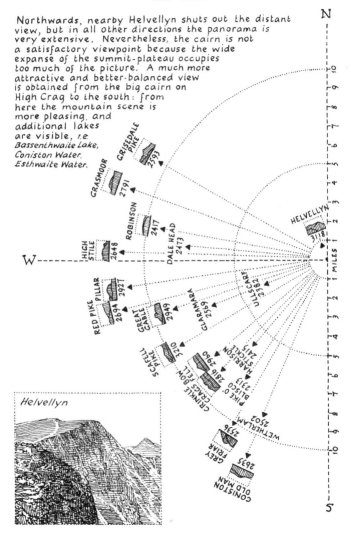

N

10
9
8
7
6
5
4
3
2
1

W — MILES — 1 2 3 4 5 6 7 8 9 10

S

GRISEDALE PIKE 2593

GRASMOOR 2791

ROBINSON 2417

HIGH STILE 2648

DALE HEAD 2473

HELVELLYN 3118

RED PIKE 2707
PILLAR 2927

GREAT GABLE 2949

GLARAMARA 2569

ULLSCARF 2382

SCAFELL 3210

CRINKLE CRAGS 2816
BOWFELL 2960

HARRISON STICKLE 2415

PIKE O' BLISCO 2313

WETHERLAM 2502

GREY FRIAR 2536

CONISTON OLD MAN 2635

Helvellyn

THE VIEW

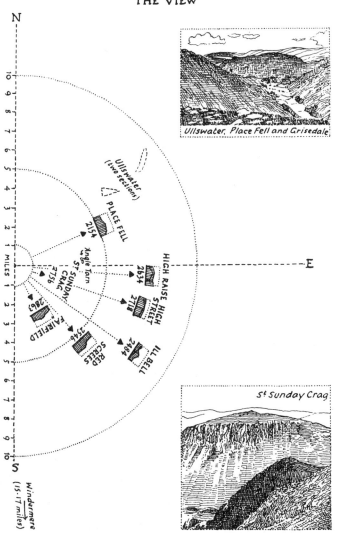

N

10
9
8
7
6
5
4
3
2
1
MILES

E

S

Ullswater
(two sections)

PLACE FELL
2154

Angle Tarn
ST SUNDAY
CRAG
2756

HIGH RAISE
2634

HIGH STREET
2718

FAIRFIELD
2863

RED
SCREES
2746

ILL BELL
2484

Windermere
(15-17 miles)

Ullswater, Place Fell and Grisedale

St Sunday Crag

Raise

2897'

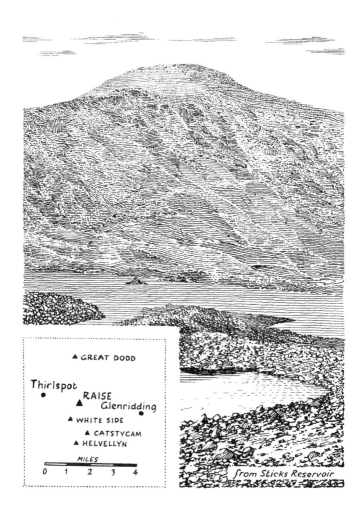

▲ GREAT DODD

Thirlspot
●

▲ RAISE
    Glenridding
       ●

▲ WHITE SIDE

▲ CATSTYCAM

▲ HELVELLYN

MILES

0 1 2 3 4

from Sticks Reservoir

NATURAL FEATURES

Raise deserves a special cheer. It is the only summit in the Helvellyn range adorned with a crown of rough rocks — and they make a welcome change from the dull monotony of the green expanses around Sticks Pass. But in general the fell conforms to the usual Helvellyn pattern, the western slopes being grassy and the eastern slopes more scarred. It further differs from its fellows on the main ridge, however, in that its western slopes do not reach down to the valley: they are sandwiched between the more extensive, sprawling flanks of Stybarrow Dodd and White Side and are crowded out completely at the 1600' contour.

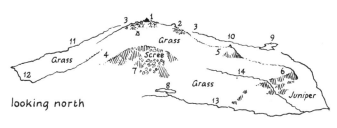

looking north

1 : The summit
2 : Rock tor
3 : Sticks Pass
4 : Ridge continuing to White Side
5 : Stang
6 : Stang End
7 : Keppel Cove

8 : Keppelcove Tarn (dry)
9 : Sticks Reservoir (dry)
10 : Sticks Gill (East)
11 : Sticks Gill (West)
12 : Brund Gill
13 : Glenridding Beck
14 : Rowten Beck

The Rock Tor

This small outcrop rises
from a slope of lichened scree.
It is not remarkable in itself, but
stands out so prominently that it forms
a ready means of identifying Raise in
all views where the east slope is seen in profile.

MAP

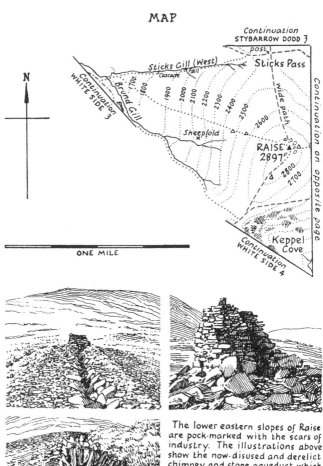

Continuation STYBARROW DODD 3

N

Sticks Gill (West)
Fall
Cascade
Sticks Pass
post
wide path

Continuation WHITE SIDE 3

Brund Gill

1700
1800
1900
2000
2100
2200
2300
2400
2500
2600

Continuation on opposite page

Sheepfold

RAISE
2897

2800
2700

Continuation WHITE SIDE 4

Keppel Cove

ONE MILE

The lower eastern slopes of Raise are pock-marked with the scars of industry. The illustrations above show the now-disused and derelict chimney and stone aqueduct which formerly served the Glenridding lead mine. Only a small portion of the aqueduct remains intact (see picture on left) but it is sufficient to indicate the skill of the masons who built it and to make one envy their pride in the job, and be glad they are not here to see the ruins.

MAP

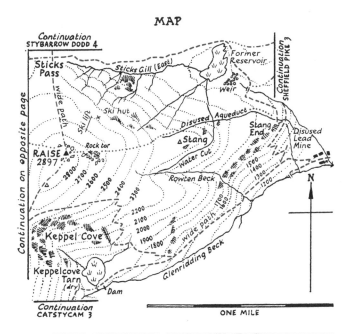

Continuation
STYBARROW DODD 4

Continuation
SHEFFIELD PIKE 3

Sticks
Pass

Sticks Gill (East)

Former
Reservoir

Weir

Continuation on opposite page

Wide Path

Ski lift

Ski hut

Disused Aqueduct

Stang
End

Disused
Lead
Mine

Stang

Water Cut

RAISE
2897

Rock tor

Rowten Beck

N

2800 2700 2600 2500 2400 2300 2200 2100 2000 1900 1800

1500 1400 1300 1200

1700 1600

Keppel Cove

wide path

Glenridding Beck

Keppelcove
Tarn
(dry)

Dam

Continuation
CATSTYCAM 3

ONE MILE

Glenridding and Ullswater, from Stang End

ASCENTS FROM STANAH AND THIRLSPOT
2400 feet of ascent : 2½ miles

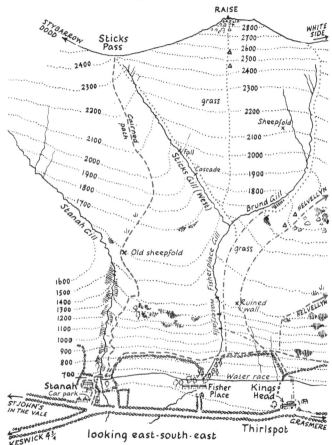

looking east-south-east

Raise overlooks Sticks Pass, from which it is climbed very easily; the path from Stanah to the top of the pass is therefore a convenient route of ascent. Routes from Thirlspot are more direct but lack paths much of the way. All the western approaches are grassy and rather dull.

ASCENT FROM GLENRIDDING
2500 feet of ascent : 4 miles from Glenridding village

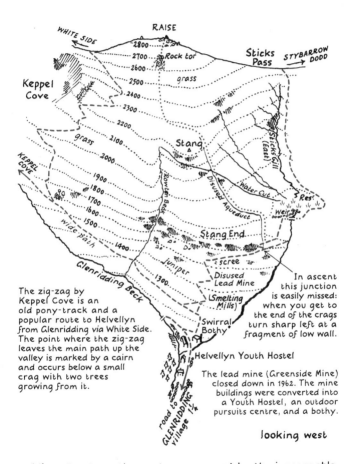

RAISE

WHITE SIDE

2800
2700 · Rock tor
2600
2500
2400 grass
2300
2200
2100
2000
1900
1800
1700
1500
1400
1300

Keppel Cove

Sticks Pass → STYBARROW DODD

Stang

Sticks Gill (East)

Disused Aqueduct

Water Cut

Rest

Weir

Stang End

scree

Disused Lead Mine

(Smelting Mills)

Swirral Bothy

Glenridding Beck

Juniper

wide path

KEPPEL COVE

grass

Rowten Beck

looking west

The zig-zag by Keppel Cove is an old pony-track and a popular route to Helvellyn from Glenridding via White Side. The point where the zig-zag leaves the main path up the valley is marked by a cairn and occurs below a small crag with two trees growing from it.

In ascent this junction is easily missed: when you get to the end of the crags turn sharp left at a fragment of low wall.

Helvellyn Youth Hostel

road to GLENRIDDING village 1½

The lead mine (Greenside Mine) closed down in 1962. The mine buildings were converted into a Youth Hostel, an outdoor pursuits centre, and a bothy.

All routes from the east are marred by the inescapable evidences of the lead mine. The Keppel Cove route is easy, and gives impressive views of Catstycam. The approach by Sticks Pass is dull, that by the old aqueduct rather better.

THE SUMMIT

SKIDDAW

The summit is a level grassy plateau, capped at its higher end by an outcrop of very rough gnarled stones. The main cairn takes the form of a wind-shelter facing north. Smaller cairns on nearby rocks indicate other viewpoints.

DESCENTS: In good weather all routes of ascent are suitable also for descent. The quickest way to Thirlspot is down the western slope, joining a path by Fisher Gill. For Glenridding, the route by the old aqueduct is quickest; if the zig-zag by Keppel Cove is preferred, a big corner may be saved initially by descending to it south-east from the summit.
In bad conditions, head for the *top* of Sticks Pass, north, whatever the destination.
In mist, remember that the wind-shelter faces north.

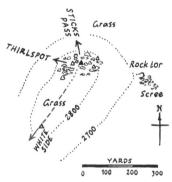

STICKS PASS

Grass

THIRLSPOT

Rock tor

Scree

Grass

2800

WHITE SIDE

2700

N

YARDS

0   100   200   300

BIRKHOUSE MOOR

The summit of Stang

RIDGE ROUTES

To STYBARROW DODD, 2770' : 1 mile : N, then NE
Depression at 2420' (Sticks Pass)
350 feet of ascent
Grass all the way after initial stones. Easy.
Distinct path. Safe in mist.

Cross Sticks Pass at its highest point, and
continue up the steepening slope opposite.
The cairn on the south-west top is usually
accepted as the summit of Stybarrow Dodd,
but there is higher ground beyond.

To WHITE SIDE, 2832' : ¾ mile : SW

*Depression
at 2650.'
200 feet
of ascent.*

*Over rocks at
first. Then easy
walking on well
cairned path.*

Cross the summit-plateau to the south-
west cairn and descend therefrom to
the good path coming up on the left: it
climbs easily to the top of White Side.

HALF A MILE

This slope is a favourite with
skiers and, on snowy winter
days, presents an animated
scene : a ski-lift operates.

Raise from Sticks Pass

THE VIEW

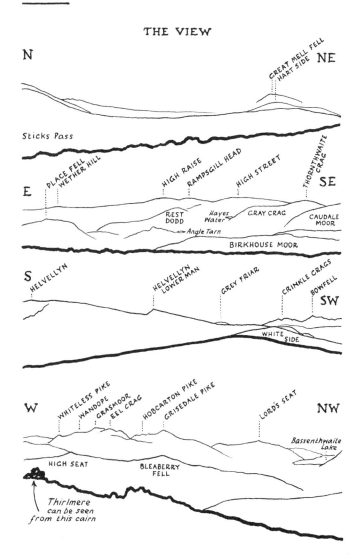

THE VIEW

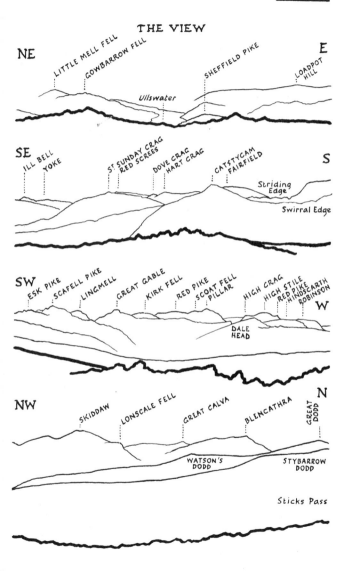

NE — LITTLE MELL FELL — COWBARROW FELL — Ullswater — SHEFFIELD PIKE — LOADPOT HILL — E

SE — ILL BELL — YOKE — ST SUNDAY CRAG — RED SCREES — DOVE CRAG — HART CRAG — CATSTYCAM — FAIRFIELD — Striding Edge — Swirral Edge — S

SW — ESK PIKE — SCAFELL PIKE — LINGMELL — GREAT GABLE — KIRK FELL — RED PIKE — SCOAT FELL — PILLAR — DALE HEAD — HIGH CRAG — HIGH STILE — RED PIKE — HINDSCARTH — ROBINSON — W

NW — SKIDDAW — LONSCALE FELL — GREAT CALVA — WATSON'S DODD — BLENCATHRA — STYBARROW DODD — GREAT DODD — N

Sticks Pass

Red Screes

2546'

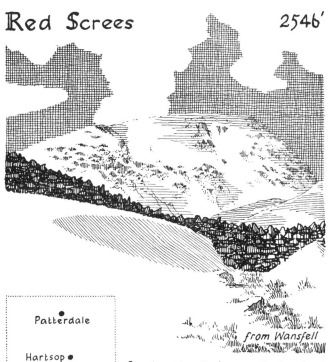

from Wansfell

Patterdale

Hartsop ●

▲ DOVE CRAG

▲
RED SCREES

● Ambleside

MILES
0   1   2   3

Prominent in all views of the Lakeland fells from the lesser heights of South Westmorland is the high whale-backed mass of Red Screes, rising in a graceful curve from the head of Windermere and descending abruptly at its northern end. Some maps append the name 'Kilnshaw Chimney' to the summit, but Red Screes is its name by popular choice—and Red Screes it should be because of the colour and character of its eastern face. It is a friendly accommodating hill, holding no terrors for those who climb to its summit by the usual easy routes and being very conveniently situated for sojourners at Ambleside; moreover, it offers a reward of excellent views.

NATURAL FEATURES

All travellers along the Kirkstone Pass are familiar with Red Screes, for it is the biggest thing to be seen there: for four miles it forms the western wall of the pass. In general structure it is a long broad ridge of considerable bulk. The southern slopes are at an easy gradient, with rock outcrops in abundance and a quarry which produces beautiful green stone; in places the rough ground steepens into crags. The shorter north ridge, after a gradual descent to the lesser height of Middle Dodd, plunges steeply to the fields of High Hartsop. The western slopes are of no particular interest and the pride of Red Screes is undoubtedly its eastern face, where natural forces have eroded two combes which carve deeply into the mountain on both flanks of a wide buttress: runs of fine red scree pour down these hollows. This side of the fell has many crags and tumbled boulders, one of which gave the pass its name; high up is Kilnshaw Chimney, which is hardly as significant as the maps would imply, being only a narrow gully choked with scree.

Red Screes, although in the midst of high country, contrives to appear more isolated from its fellows than any other of the eastern fells. It is independent and is unsupported, not buttressed by its neighbours: to this extent, it may be said to have the purest mountain form among the eastern fells.

Of the many streams which have their birth on Red Screes, the best-known is Stock Ghyll, flowing south and breaking in lovely waterfalls on its way to join the Rothay; on the west, innumerable watercourses feed Scandale Beck; northwards, Kirkstone Beck and Caiston Beck carry its waters to Ullswater.

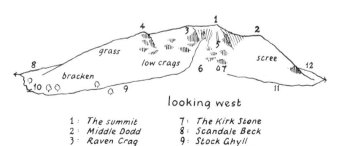

looking west

1 : The summit
2 : Middle Dodd
3 : Raven Crag
4 : Snarker Pike
5 : Kilnshaw Chimney
6 : Kirkstone Pass
7 : The Kirk Stone
8 : Scandale Beck
9 : Stock Ghyll
10 : Stock Ghyll Force
11 : Kirkstone Beck
12 : Caiston Beck

MAP

Continuation on opposite page

ONE MILE

MAP

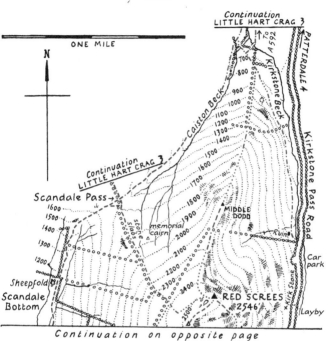

One Mile

N

Continuation
LITTLE HART CRAG 3

PATTERDALE 4

To 765

Kirkstone Beck

Caiston Beck

Kirkstone Pass Road

Continuation
LITTLE HART CRAG 3

Scandale Pass →

memorial
cairn

MIDDLE DODD

Ruin

Car
park

Sheepfold

Scandale
Bottom

Kirk Stone

▲ RED SCREES
2546'

Layby

Continuation on opposite page

The Kirk Stone

This fallen boulder stands about sixty yards to the left (west) of the road at the top of the steep descent to the north. It is a prominent object on the way up the pass from Brothers Water, having the appearance of a ridged church-tower.

ASCENT FROM AMBLESIDE
2400 feet of ascent : 4 or 5 miles

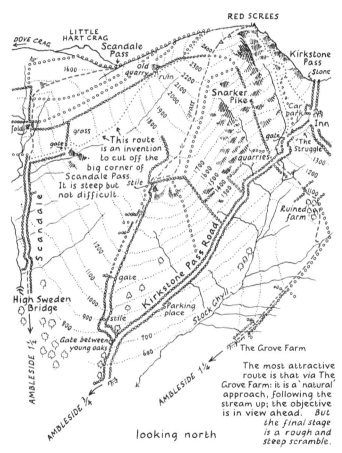

RED SCREES

DOVE CRAG

LITTLE HART CRAG

Scandale Pass

Kirkstone Pass
Stone

1600
old quarry
ruin
2400
2300
2200
2100
2000
1900
1800
grass

Snarker Pike

Car park

Inn

fold
grass
gate
←This route
is an invention
to cut off the
big corner of
Scandale Pass.
It is steep but
not difficult.
stile

gate
The Struggle
1300
quarries
1700
1600
1500
1400
1300
1200

Scandale

Kirkstone Pass Road

Ruined farm

1200

1100
1000
900
800
High Sweden Bridge
gate
stile
Parking place
Stock Chyll

Gate between young oaks
700
600

The Grove Farm

AMBLESIDE 1½

AMBLESIDE ¾

AMBLESIDE 1¼

The most attractive
route is that via The
Grove Farm: it is a 'natural'
approach, following the
stream up; the objective
is in view ahead. *But
the final stage
is a rough and
steep scramble.*

looking north

Of the routes shown, two only are commonly in use:
the direct ridge route (which is better in descending)
and the longer Scandale Pass route (the safest in bad
weather). The best 'round tour' is to ascend by way of
The Grove Farm and return by descending the ridge.

ASCENT FROM PATTERDALE
2200 feet of ascent : 6½ miles from Patterdale village

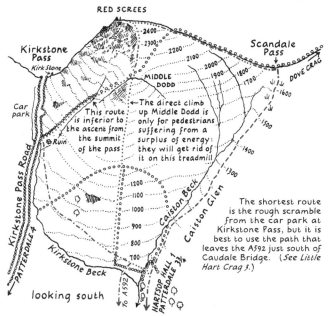

RED SCREES

Kirkstone Pass

Kirk Stone

Car park

Ruin

MIDDLE DODD

Scandale Pass

DOVE CRAG

This route is inferior to the ascent from the summit of the pass

← The direct climb up Middle Dodd is only for pedestrians suffering from a surplus of energy: they will get rid of it on this treadmill

The shortest route is the rough scramble from the car park at Kirkstone Pass, but it is best to use the path that leaves the A592 just south of Caudale Bridge. (*See Little Hart Crag 3*.)

Caiston Beck

Caiston Glen

Kirkstone Beck

Kirkstone Pass Road

PATTERDALE

looking south

TO A592

HARTSOP HALL

PATTERDALE 1

PATTERDALE 3½

2400 2300 2200 2100 2000 1900 1800 1700 1600 1500 1400 1300 1200 1100 1000 900 800 700

The approach from Patterdale is very fine, but a little road-walking, both going and returning, robs the journey of some of its charm; alternatives along the valley can be found, however. The popular route is by Caiston Glen.

looking down on the Kirkstone Pass Inn

THE SUMMIT

The summit is a large grassy plateau, having three principal cairns widely spaced and differing little in altitude. There is no mistaking the highest, a huge mound of stones situated at the extreme corner of the plateau: a dramatic site, for here the ground seems to collapse at one's feet and plunge steeply down to the winding road far below. An Ordnance Survey column stands alongside, and twenty yards west is a small tarn with another to the south-west of it. Below and east of the highest cairn is a prominent cluster of rocks worth visiting: it is a good vantage point and a pleasant place to eat sandwiches if the top is crowded, but it is well to tread cautiously here: beware crag!

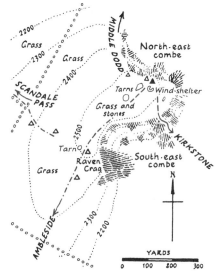

DESCENTS: The best way down to Ambleside is by the south ridge — it is so easy a saunter that the hands need be taken from the pockets only to negotiate gates and stiles. Also easy, but longer, is the Scandale Pass route. The direct descent to Kirkstone is rough, too rough to be enjoyable.

For Patterdale, the way over Middle Dodd is excellent, but steep. The Caiston Glen path is easy, but descents to Kirkstone are not recommended, except for the *very* thirsty.

In bad weather, the safest course of all is to aim for the top of Scandale Pass — for either Ambleside or Patterdale.

Patterdale, from the summit

N

2000 ▲ LITTLE
HART CRAG

1900
Tarn

Scandale
Pass →

1800

1700

QUARTER
MILE

1700

1800

1900

2000

2100

2200

2300

2400

1500

▲ RED
SCREES

Red Screes
has no high
connecting link
with any other
major fell. On the
Fairfield round, the
next adjacent fell
is Little Hart Crag

RIDGE ROUTE

To LITTLE HART CRAG, 2091': 1¼ miles
W, then NW and E

Depression at 1675'
430 feet of ascent

An easy and tedious walk.

On grass, following the wall
across Scandale Pass. Little
Hart Crag is not safe in mist

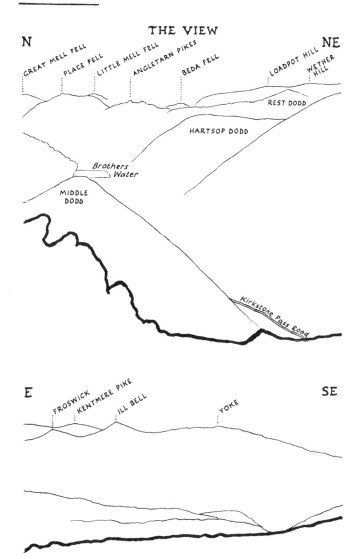

THE VIEW

THE VIEW

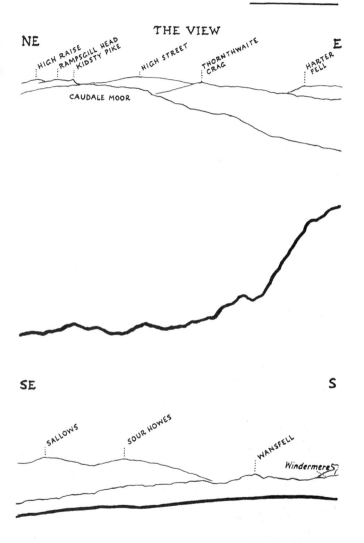

NE

HIGH RAISE
RAMPSGILL HEAD
KIDSTY PIKE

HIGH STREET

THORNTHWAITE
CRAG

HARTER
FELL

E

CAUDALE MOOR

SE

SALLOWS

SOUR HOWES

WANSFELL

Windermere

S

continued

THE VIEW

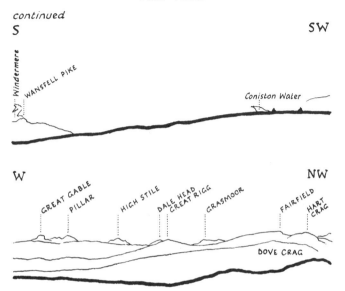

continued

S — SW

Windermere
WANSFELL PIKE
Coniston Water

W — NW

GREAT GABLE
PILLAR
HIGH STILE
DALE HEAD
GREAT RIGG
CRASMOOR
FAIRFIELD
HART CRAG
DOVE CRAG

The south-east combe

The north-east combe

THE VIEW

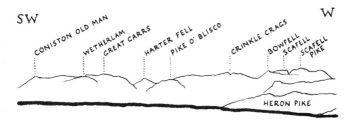

SW — W

CONISTON OLD MAN · WETHERLAM · GREAT CARRS · HARTER FELL · PIKE O' BLISCO · CRINKLE CRAGS · BOWFELL · SCAFELL · SCAFELL PIKE

HERON PIKE

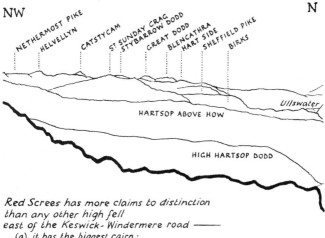

NW — N

NETHERMOST PIKE · HELVELLYN · CATSTYCAM · ST SUNDAY CRAG · STYBARROW DODD · GREAT DODD · BLENCATHRA · HART SIDE · SHEFFIELD PIKE · BIRKS

Ullswater

HARTSOP ABOVE HOW

HIGH HARTSOP DODD

*Red Screes has more claims to distinction
than any other high fell
east of the Keswick-Windermere road* ——

  (a) *it has the biggest cairn;*
  (b) *it has the greatest mileage of stone walls;*
  (c) *it has one of the highest sheets of permanent standing water, and,
     in springtime, the highest resident population of tadpoles;*
  (d) *it has the purest mountain form;*
  (e) *it has the reddest screes and the greenest stone;*
  (f) *it has one of the finest views (but not the most extensive nor the
     most beautiful) and the finest of the High Street range;*
  (g) *it has the easiest way down;*
  (h) *it offers alcoholic beverages at 1480';*
  (i) *it gives birth to the stream with the most beautiful waterfalls.*
    *[Some of these statements are expressions of opinion;
              others, especially (h), are hard facts]*

Saint Sunday Crag 2756'

Glenridding
Patterdale
▲ HELVELLYN
ST SUNDAY
CRAG ▲
Hartsop
▲ FAIRFIELD

MILES
0   1   2   3   4

from Ullswater

NATURAL FEATURES

The slender soaring lines of St Sunday Crag and its aloof height and steepness endow this fine mountain with special distinction. It stands on a triangular base and its sides rise with such regularity that all its contours assume the same shape, as does the final summit-plateau. Ridges ascend from the corners of the triangle to the top of the fell, the one best-defined naturally rising from the sharpest angle: this is the south-west ridge connecting with Fairfield at Deepdale Hause. A shorter rougher ridge runs down northeast to Birks. Due east of the top is a subsidiary peak, Gavel Pike, from which a broadening ridge falls to Deepdale. A fringe of crags, nearly a mile in length, overtops the Grisedale face, which drops nearly 2000 feet in height in a lateral distance of half-a-mile: in Lakeland, only Great Gable can show greater concentrated steepness over a similar fall in altitude. The south-east face is also steep but less impressive, and the easy slopes to the north-east break into foothills before dropping abruptly to valley-level in Patterdale: these slopes are the gathering grounds of Coldcove Gill, the main stream.

Every walker who aspires to high places and looks up at the remote summit of St Sunday Crag will experience an urge to go forth and climb up to it, for its challenge is very strong. Its rewards are equally generous, and altogether this is a noble fell. Saint Sunday must surely look down on his memorial with profound gratification.

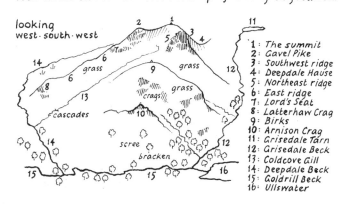

looking
west-south-west

1 : The summit
2 : Gavel Pike
3 : Southwest ridge
4 : Deepdale Hause
5 : Northeast ridge
6 : East ridge
7 : Lord's Seat
8 : Latterhaw Crag
9 : Birks
10 : Arnison Crag
11 : Grisedale Tarn
12 : Grisedale Beck
13 : Coldcove Gill
14 : Deepdale Beck
15 : Goldrill Beck
16 : Ullswater

NATURAL FEATURES

St Sunday Crag has an imposing appearance
from whatever direction it is seen, an
attribute rare in mountains. From
Ullswater and from Grisedale
its outline is very familiar;
less well known (because
less often seen) is its
fine eastern aspect.

SUMMIT

GAVEL
PIKE

LORD'S
SEAT

LATTERHAW
CRAG

The East Ridge, from Dubhow

There is a glimpse, often unnoticed, of the lofty east
ridge soaring high above Deepdale, from the roadway
near Bridgend. A much better view is obtained from
Dubhow, nearby on the old cart-track across the valley.

Cascades, Coldcove Gill

Summit of Gavel Pike

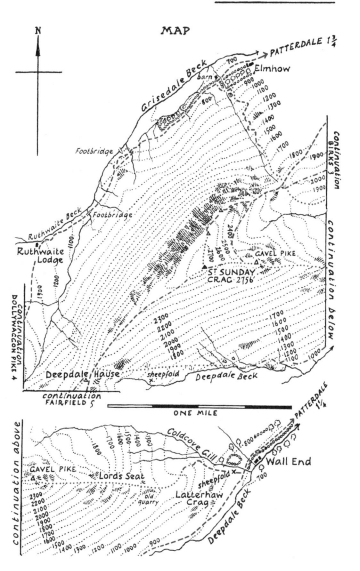

MAP

N

PATTERDALE 1¾

Grisedale Beck

700

barn

800

Elmhow

1100

1200

1300

1400

1500

1600

1800

1900

Footbridge

continuation BIRKS 3

2000

1900

Ruthwaite Beck

Footbridge

1000

1100

continuation below

2400

1200

GAVEL PIKE

2500

2600

Ruthwaite
Lodge

1700

ST SUNDAY
CRAG 2756

1200

2300

2200

2100

2000

1900

1800

1700

1600

1500

1400

1300

1200

1100

1000

continuation
DOLLYWAGGON PIKE 4

Deepdale Hause

sheepfold

Deepdale Beck

continuation
FAIRFIELD 5

ONE MILE

continuation above

PATTERDALE 1¼

Coldcove Gill

800

Wall End

GAVEL PIKE

1400

1500

1600

1700

1800

Lords Seat

sheepfold

700

2300

2200

2100

2000

1900

1800

1700

1600

1500

1400

old
quarry

Latterhaw
Crag

1300

1200

1100

1000

900

Deepdale Beck

ASCENT FROM PATTERDALE
2300 feet of ascent : 3 miles (4 by East Ridge)

looking south-west

ST SUNDAY CRAG

GAVEL PIKE

2700
2600
2500
2400
2300
2200
2100
2000
1900

East Ridge

Lord's Seat

DEEPDALE HAUSE

1800
1700
1600
1500

GRISEDALE TARN

The Elmhow zigzag, once the popular route, has now fallen from favour and is not easy to find

Latterhaw Crag

Colecove Gill

BIRKS

ruin x

grass

grass

bracken

Black Crag

scree
bracken

barn

Elmhow

bracken

Grisedale Beck

Thornhow End

1100
1000
900
800

sheepfold

900
800

Trough Head

1300

stile

1200

Hag Beck

Glenamara Park

Wall End

1300
1200
1000

bracken
1000

scree

ARNISON CRAG

bracken

gate

Deepdale Beck

Further details of Arnison Crag and Birks will be found in the separate chapters on those fells.

900

800

Mill Moss

Church

car park

Deepdale Hall

gate

Patterdale

parking place

KIRKSTONE ←

parking place

Bridgend

The *easiest* route (not depicted) follows Deepdale to its head at Deepdale Hause, then ascends the southwest ridge. Apart from a short sharp pull on to the Hause there is no steep climbing. There are intimate views of the crags of Fairfield

The popular route is *via* Thornhow End and the western flank of Birks (in clear weather it is better to proceed over the top of Birks). The Trough Head route is easier but dull. The east ridge is an interesting alternative and technically the best line of ascent.

ASCENT FROM GRISEDALE TARN
1000 feet of ascent : 1¾ miles

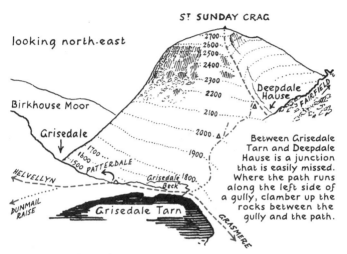

looking north-east

ST SUNDAY CRAG

2700
2600
2500
2400
2300
2200
2100
2000

Deepdale
Hause

FAIRFIELD

Birkhouse Moor

Grisedale

1900

1700
1600
1500 PATTERDALE

HELVELLYN

Grisedale 1800
Beck

DUNMAIL
RAISE

Grisedale Tarn

GRASMERE
GRASMERE

Between Grisedale
Tarn and Deepdale
Hause is a junction
that is easily missed.
Where the path runs
along the left side of
a gully, clamber up the
rocks between the
gully and the path.

St Sunday Crag is commonly and correctly regarded
as the preserve of Patterdale, yet it is interesting to
note that the summit is less than three miles from
the Keswick-Ambleside road at Dunmail Raise : it
may be ascended easily and quickly from here. And
from Grasmere via Tongue Gill.   In either case, the
first objective is Grisedale Tarn.

St Sunday Crag
from Grisedale Tarn

THE SUMMIT

The summit hardly lives up to the promise of the ridges: it is merely a slight stony mound set on the edge of a plateau — a pleasant place of mosses and lichens and grey rocks, but quite unexciting. Two cairns adorn the top, and there is also a well-built column of stones a quarter of a mile away across the plateau to the north.

Gavel Pike has a much more attractive summit than the main fell: here are bilberries and heather and natural armchairs among the rocks of the tiny peaked top, and splendid views to enjoy. A delectable place for (packed) lunch!

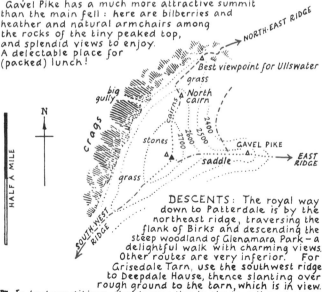

DESCENTS: The royal way down to Patterdale is by the northeast ridge, traversing the flank of Birks and descending the steep woodland of Glenamara Park — a delightful walk with charming views. Other routes are very inferior. For Grisedale Tarn, use the southwest ridge to Deepdale Hause, thence slanting over rough ground to the tarn, which is in view.

In bad conditions, the danger lies in the long line of crags on the Grisedale face, this fortunately being preceded by steep ground which serves as a warning. For Patterdale, the path from the saddle is safest.

Ullswater
from the
north-east ridge

RIDGE ROUTES

To FAIRFIELD, 2863' : 1½ miles : SW then S
Depression at 2150' : 750 feet of ascent
A simple descent followed by rough scrambling

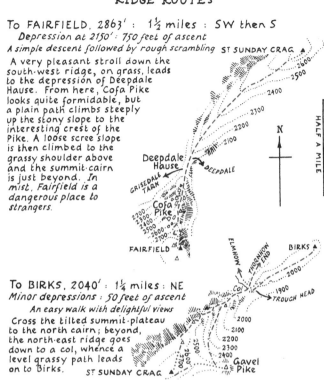

A very pleasant stroll down the south-west ridge, on grass, leads to the depression of Deepdale Hause. From here, Cofa Pike looks quite formidable, but a plain path climbs steeply up the stony slope to the interesting crest of the Pike. A loose scree slope is then climbed to the grassy shoulder above and the summit-cairn is just beyond. *In mist, Fairfield is a dangerous place to strangers.*

To BIRKS, 2040' : 1¼ miles : NE
Minor depressions : 50 feet of ascent
An easy walk with delightful views

Cross the tilted summit-plateau to the north cairn; beyond, the north-east ridge goes down to a col, whence a level grassy path leads on to Birks.

The view from the north cairn

THE VIEW

Principal Fells

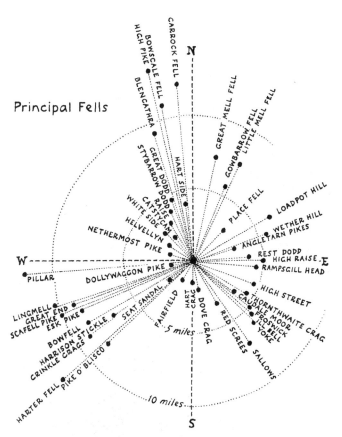

The walker who reaches the summit eagerly expecting to see the classic view of Ullswater from St Sunday Crag will be disappointed — he must go to the bristly rocks at the top of the north-east ridge for that. The lake makes a beautiful picture also from the saddle leading to Gavel Pike. Helvellyn is a fine study in mountain structure, and the best aspect of Fairfield is seen, but these two fells restrict the view. The High Street range, however, is well seen.

Lakes and Tarns
NE : *Ullswater*
E : *Angle Tarn*

Seat Sandal 2415'

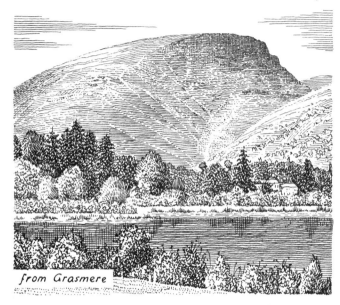

from Grasmere

HELVELLYN
▲

FAIRFIELD
▲
SEAT SANDAL ▲

Grasmere
●

MILES
0   1   2

Cascade, Raise Beck

NATURAL FEATURES

Prominent in the Grasmere landscape is the lofty outline of Seat Sandal, soaring gracefully from Dunmail Raise to the flat-topped summit and then suddenly falling away in a steep plunge eastwards. This view reveals its character well: the western flanks are smooth curves of grass and bracken, but the eastern face is a rough slope of shattered cliff and tumbled rock and loose scree from which rises abruptly an overhanging crag. Seat Sandal is a simple straightforward fell, uninteresting except as a viewpoint, with no dramatic effects, no hidden surprises. Geographically it belongs to Fairfield, to which it is connected by a low ridge crossed by the Grisedale Pass.

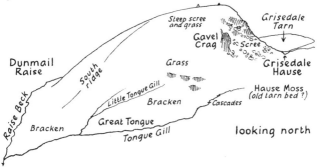

Steep scree and grass

Grisedale Tarn

Gavel Crag

Scree

Dunmail Raise

South ridge

Grass

Grisedale Hause

Little Tongue Gill

Bracken

Cascades

Hause Moss (old tarn bed ?)

Raise Beck

Bracken

Great Tongue

Tongue Gill

looking north

Seat Sandal has one distinction: its waters reach the sea at more widely divergent points than those of any other Lakeland fell. This has been so since the diversion of Raise Beck to feed Thirlmere. (*Dollywaggon Pike shares this distinction only when Raise Beck is flowing south at Dunmail Raise*)

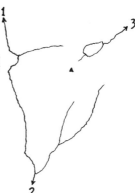

1 : Raise Beck —
    to Thirlmere and (that which escapes being sent back south over Dunmail to Manchester) via Derwentwater to the sea at Workington.

2 : Raise Beck and Tongue Gill —
    to Grasmere, Windermere and Morecambe Bay.

3 : Grisedale Beck —
    to Ullswater and the Solway Firth.

MAP

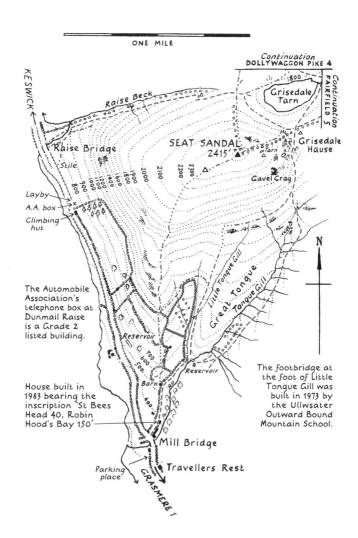

ONE MILE

Continuation
DOLLYWAGGON PIKE 4

Continuation
FAIRFIELD 5

KESWICK

Raise Beck

Grisedale
Tarn

Raise Bridge

SEAT SANDAL
2415'

Grisedale
Hause

Stile

Tarn

Layby

Gavel Crag

A.A. box

Climbing
hut

The Automobile
Association's
telephone box at
Dunmail Raise
is a Grade 2
listed building.

Little Tongue Gill

Great Tongue

Tongue Gill

N

Reservoir

House built in
1983 bearing the
inscription 'St Bees
Head 40, Robin
Hood's Bay 150'

Reservoir

Barn

The footbridge at
the foot of Little
Tongue Gill was
built in 1973 by
the Ullswater
Outward Bound
Mountain School.

Mill Bridge

Travellers Rest

Parking
place

GRASMERE 1

ASCENT FROM GRASMERE
2200 feet of ascent : 3¼ miles from Grasmere Church

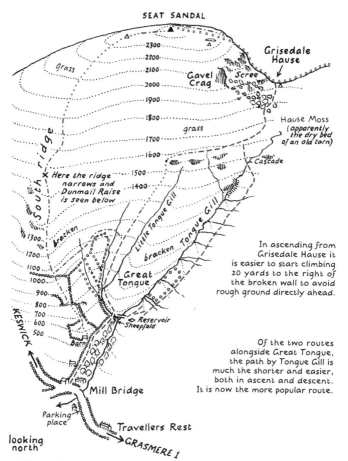

SEAT SANDAL

Grisedale Hause

grass

2300
2200
2100
2000
1900
1800
1700
1600
1500
1400

Gavel Crag

Scree

Hause Moss
(apparently
the dry bed
of an old tarn)

grass

Cascade

South ridge

✕ Here the ridge
narrows and
Dunmail Raise
is seen below

1300
1200
1100
1000
900
800
700
600
500

bracken

Little Tongue Gill

Tongue Gill

bracken

Great
Tongue

In ascending from
Grisedale Hause it
is easier to start climbing
20 yards to the right of
the broken wall to avoid
rough ground directly ahead.

KESWICK

Reservoir
Sheepfold

Of the two routes
alongside Great Tongue,
the path by Tongue Gill is
much the shorter and easier,
both in ascent and descent.
It is now the more popular route.

Barn

Mill Bridge

Parking
place

Travellers Rest

GRASMERE 1

looking
north

The path to Grisedale Hause, keeping right of the Tongue,
is distinct, but there is no continuous path above the Hause
or along the south ridge. If returning to Grasmere it would
be better to ascend by the Hause and descend by the ridge.

ASCENT FROM DUNMAIL RAISE
1700 feet of ascent : 1½ miles

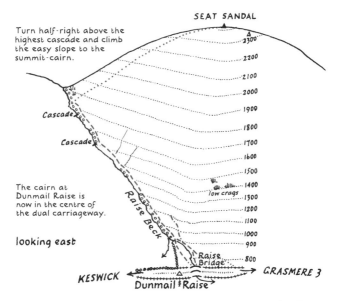

SEAT SANDAL

Turn half-right above the highest cascade and climb the easy slope to the summit-cairn.

2300
2200
2100
2000
1900
1800
1700
1600
1500
1400
low crags
1300
1200
1100
1000
900
800

Cascade

Cascade

Raise Beck

The cairn at Dunmail Raise is now in the centre of the dual carriageway.

looking east

Raise Bridge

KESWICK ← | → GRASMERE 3
Dunmail Raise

Seat Sandal is very easily climbed from Raise Bridge. The direct route by the shoulder is not recommended: it is preferable to commence the ascent by using the rough path alongside the beck. This is a quick way up.

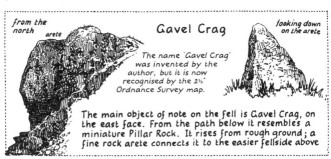

from the north arete

looking down on the arete

Gavel Crag

The name 'Gavel Crag' was invented by the author, but it is now recognised by the 2½" Ordnance Survey map.

The main object of note on the fell is Gavel Crag, on the east face. From the path below it resembles a miniature Pillar Rock. It rises from rough ground; a fine rock arete connects it to the easier fellside above

THE SUMMIT

The summit is a flat grassy plateau with small stony outcrops. A broken wall crosses the top. The main cairn stands 30 yards west of the wall; two other cairns indicate alternative viewpoints.

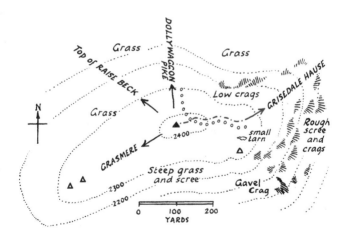

DESCENTS : The best way off the summit, in clear weather, is by the south ridge to Grasmere, the views being excellent and the gradient exactly right — this is one of the quickest descents in the district. All routes are safe in good conditions. The east face is steep, and should be avoided.

In bad weather conditions, the safest descent is to Grisedale Hause (by the wall) where good paths lead to Grasmere and Patterdale.

THE VIEW

Principal Fells

Most of the interest in the view
is in the western arc, where the
panorama is excellent. In other
directions, nearby Helvellyn and
Fairfield limit the distant view.
Many lakes and tarns are visible.

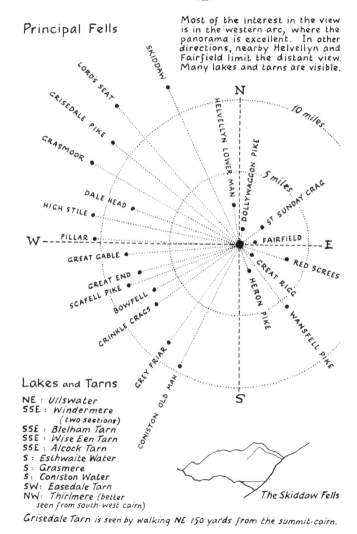

Lakes and Tarns

NE : Ullswater
SSE : Windermere
 (two sections)
SSE : Blelham Tarn
SSE : Wise Een Tarn
SSE : Alcock Tarn
S : Esthwaite Water
S : Grasmere
S : Coniston Water
SW : Easedale Tarn
NW : Thirlmere (better
 seen from south-west cairn)

The Skiddaw Fells

Grisedale Tarn is seen by walking NE 150 yards from the summit-cairn.

RIDGE ROUTES

To FAIRFIELD, 2863' : 1⅓ miles : E then NE and E
Depression at 1929' : 950 feet of ascent

A rough descent followed by a steep continuous climb. The top of Fairfield is confusing and dangerous in mist to anyone who is not familiar with it, but there is no difficulty in clear weather.

The wall is a guide down to Grisedale Hause: the last part of the descent is rough but there is easier ground just to the left. The wall continues up the shoulder of Fairfield to 2400' and gives up the struggle but the determined walker toils on along a fair path. The final part of the climb, much easier but without a path, follows a line of cairns across grass to the stony top.

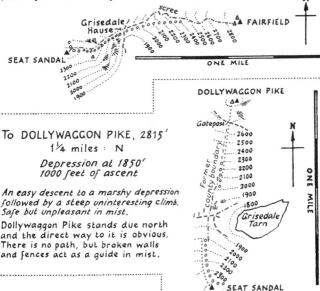

To DOLLYWAGGON PIKE, 2815'
1¼ miles : N
Depression at 1850'
1000 feet of ascent

An easy descent to a marshy depression followed by a steep uninteresting climb. Safe but unpleasant in mist.

Dollywaggon Pike stands due north and the direct way to it is obvious. There is no path, but broken walls and fences act as a guide in mist.

Ullswater from Seat Sandal

Sheffield Pike 2215'

from Glenridding

GREAT DODD ▲

Glencoyne ●

SHEFFIELD PIKE ▲
Glenridding ●

▲
HELVELLYN

Patterdale ●

MILES

0   1   2   3   4   5

NATURAL FEATURES

Stybarrow Dodd, on the main Helvellyn watershed, has a long eastern shoulder falling in stages to the shore of Ullswater. Midway, the shoulder rises to a distinct and isolated summit: this is Sheffield Pike, which assumes the characteristics of a separate fell. It soars abruptly between the valleys of Glenridding and Glencoyne and it presents to each a continuous fringe of steep crags. The eastern aspect is pleasing, with rock and heather and an occasional rowan mingling above the well-wooded slopes, but westwards the fell is drab and, in the environs of an old lead mine, downright ugly. Since the closing of the mine in 1962, the whole area has been immaculately restored. Tips are partially grass-covered and all the buildings have been demolished or put to new uses. Students of old mine workings will find little of interest here.

looking north-west

Heron Pike, from the east

MAP

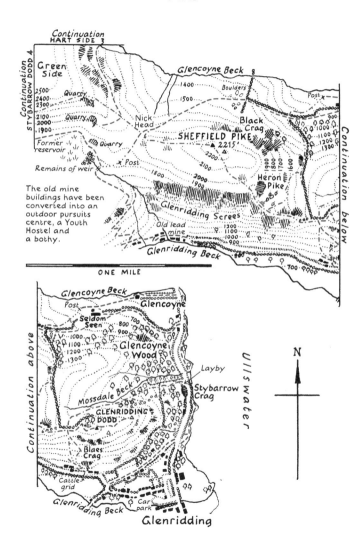

Continuation
HART SIDE 3

Continuation STYBARROW DODD 4

Green Side

2500
2400
2300
2100
2000
1900

Quarry

Quarry

Quarry

Former reservoir

Remains of weir

Post

Nick Head

Glencoyne Beck

1400

1500

Boulders

Post

900

Black Crag

SHEFFIELD PIKE ▲ 2215

2300

1800

2000
1900

Glenridding Screes

Old lead mine

1200
1100
1000
900

900

1100
1200
1300

Continuation below

1900
1800
1700
1600

Heron Pike

Glenridding Beck

700

The old mine buildings have been converted into an outdoor pursuits centre, a Youth Hostel and a bothy.

ONE MILE

Glencoyne Beck

Post

Glencoyne

Seldom Seen

800
700

1000
1100
1200
1300

Glencoyne Wood

Mossdale Beck

Layby

Stybarrow Crag

Ullswater

Continuation above

GLENRIDDING DODD

Blaes Crag

2200

Cattle grid

Glenridding Beck

Car park

Glenridding

N

ASCENT FROM GLENRIDDING
1800 feet of ascent: 2 (or 3¼) miles

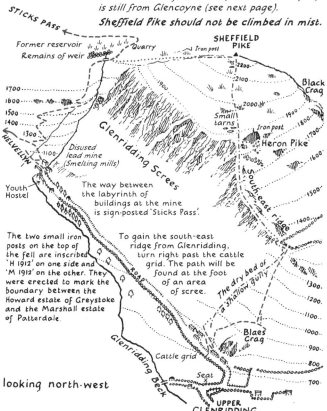

The evidences of industrialism have gone from mid-Glenridding, but the pleasantest way up is still from Glencoyne (see next page).

Sheffield Pike should not be climbed in mist.

STICKS PASS

Former reservoir
Remains of weir

Quarry

Iron post

SHEFFIELD PIKE

2200
2100
2000

Black Crag

1900
1800
1700

Small tarns

Iron post

Heron Pike

1600

Glenridding Screes

South east ridge

1500

1400

Helvellyn

1700
1600
1500
1400
1300
1100

Disused lead mine (Smelting mills)

The way between the labyrinth of buildings at the mine is sign-posted 'Sticks Pass'.

Youth Hostel

The two small iron posts on the top of the fell are inscribed 'H 1912' on one side and 'M 1912' on the other. They were erected to mark the boundary between the Howard estate of Greystoke and the Marshall estate of Patterdale.

To gain the south-east ridge from Glenridding, turn right past the cattle grid. The path will be found at the foot of an area of scree.

The dry bed of a shallow gully

1300
1200
1100
1000
900
800
700

Blaes Crag

ROAD

Cattle grid

Glenridding Beck

looking north-west

Seat
X

UPPER GLENRIDDING

Of the two routes illustrated, the climb up the ridge is much to be preferred, but it is steep and rough. The path zig-zagging above the smelting mills is longer and easier —but much less inspiring and not at all exhilarating.

ASCENT FROM GLENCOYNE
1800 feet of ascent : 2½ miles

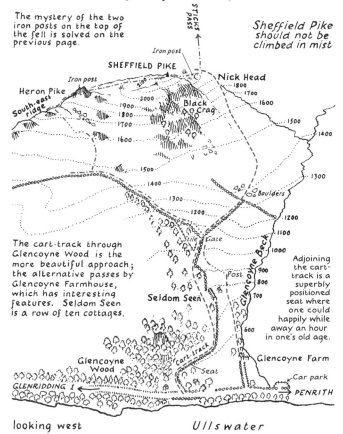

The mystery of the two iron posts on the top of the fell is solved on the previous page.

Sheffield Pike should not be climbed in mist

STICKS PASS

Iron post

SHEFFIELD PIKE

Iron post

Nick Head

Heron Pike

South-east ridge

Black Crag

2000
1900
1800
1700
1600

1800
1700
1600
1500
1400
1300

1500

1400

1300

1200

Boulders

1200

1100

1000

900
800
700

600

Stile Gate

Post

Glencoyne Beck

Seldom Seen

The cart-track through Glencoyne Wood is the more beautiful approach; the alternative passes by Glencoyne Farmhouse, which has interesting features. Seldom Seen is a row of ten cottages.

Adjoining the cart-track is a superbly positioned seat where one could happily while away an hour in one's old age.

Glencoyne Wood

Cart-track

Seat

GLENRIDDING 1

Glencoyne Farm

Car park

PENRITH

looking west

Ullswater

It is usual to follow the path to Nick Head and there turn east to the summit : this is the easiest of all ways on to the fell. Far more attractive, however, is a route traversing below Heron Pike to the top of the south-east ridge, the walking being easy and the views excellent: this is one of the pleasantest short climbs in Lakeland.

THE SUMMIT

Even on a sunny summer day the top of the fell seems a dismal place; the area above Black Crag, and the top of Heron Pike, where there is heather, are both nicer.

There are many slight undulations and craggy outcrops. Marshy ground occurs in several places and there are many small tarns.

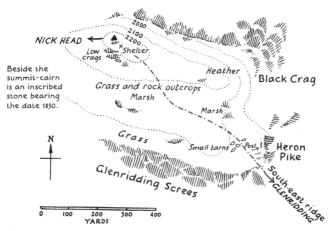

NICK HEAD ←

2000
2100
2200
Low crags   × Shelter

Beside the summit-cairn is an inscribed stone bearing the date 1830.

Grass and rock outcrops
Marsh

Heather

Black Crag

Marsh

N

Grass

Small tarns   Post

Heron Pike

Glenridding Screes

South-east ridge
GLENRIDDING

0   100   200   300   400
YARDS

DESCENTS: Any of the routes of ascent may be reversed in clear weather, the south-east ridge being incomparably the best. Some care is necessary in getting off Heron Pike on to the ridge. *There are no clear paths on the summit, which has crags on three sides.*
In bad weather conditions, the only safe way is due west to Nick Head (very gradual descent, boggy in places), from there preferably following the good path down to Glencoyne.

THE VIEW

Ullswater is the main feature
of a restricted view. Westwards
the prospect is dull; it is really
good only between north-east
and south. Heron Pike is a
much finer viewpoint.

Principal Fells

N

5 miles

2½ miles

GREAT MELL FELL
LITTLE MELL FELL
GOWBARROW FELL
GREAT DODD
HART SIDE
STYBARROW DODD
W
LOADPOT HILL
E
RAISE
PLACE FELL
WHITE SIDE
WETHER HILL
HELVELLYN LOWER MAN
CATSTYCAM
HELVELLYN
BIRKHOUSE MOOR
HIGH RAISE
FAIRFIELD
RAMPSGILL HEAD
HIGH STREET
ST. SUNDAY CRAG
THORNTHWAITE CRAG
RED SCREES
CAUDALE MOOR
S

Lakes and Tarns

NE : *Ullswater (better*
seen from the cairn
above Black Crag and
from Heron Pike)
SE : *Lanty's Tarn*
W : *Reservoir below Sticks Pass (now dry)*

Black Crag

Heron Pike

RIDGE ROUTES

To STYBARROW DODD, 2770' : 2 miles : W then NW and W.
Depression at 1925' : 1000 feet of ascent
A simple walk with a long climb on grass midway.

An easy descent westwards, boggy in places, leads to Nick Head. Cross the indistinct paths here and climb the long grassy slope ahead to the cairn on Green Side. Stybarrow Dodd is then in view in front, across a shallow depression. *This route is not recommended in bad conditions.*

To GLENRIDDING DODD, 1450': 1 mile: SE then E
Depression at 1350'
150 feet of ascent

A rough but pleasant walk; fine views

Aim for Heron Pike, 600 yards south-east, and skirt its far side (a little scrambling is necessary) to the ridge below, which continues to the rising heathery slopes of Glenridding Dodd

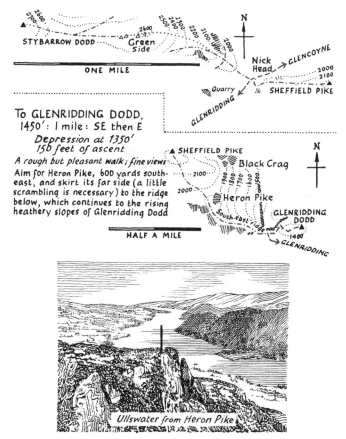

Ullswater from Heron Pike

Stone Arthur

1652'

sometimes referred to as Arthur's Chair

from Grasmere

▲ FAIRFIELD

▲ GREAT RIGG

▲ STONE ARTHUR

▲ HERON PIKE

Grasmere ● ▲ NAB SCAR

● Rydal

Ambleside ●

MILES
0 1 2 3 4

Without its prominent tor of steep rock, Stone Arthur would probably never have been given a name for it is merely the abrupt end of a spur of Great Rigg although it has the appearance of a separate fell when seen from Grasmere. The outcrop occurs where the gradual decline of the spur becomes pronounced and here are the short walls of rock, like a ruined castle, that give Stone Arthur its one touch of distinction.

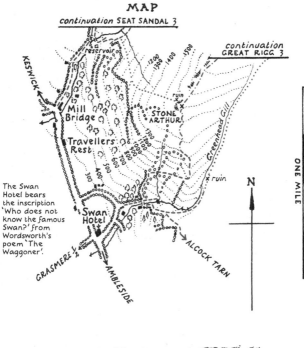

MAP

continuation SEAT SANDAL 3

continuation GREAT RIGG 3

reservoir

KESWICK

Mill Bridge

Travellers Rest

STONE ARTHUR

ruin

Greenhead Gill

ruin

The Swan Hotel bears the inscription 'Who does not know the famous Swan?' from Wordsworth's poem 'The Waggoner'.

Swan Hotel

N

ONE MILE

GRASMERE ½

AMBLESIDE

ALCOCK TARN

Grasmere, from the summit

THE VIEW

The gem of the view is Easedale Tarn in its wild setting among colourful fells with a towering background culminating in Scafell Pike. The vale of Grasmere, below, is also attractive. The southern ridge of Fairfield occupies the whole horizon to the east, uninterestingly.

Principal Fells

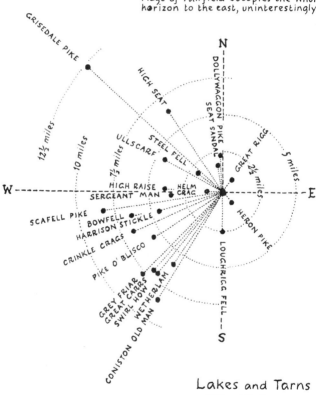

Lakes and Tarns

SSE : Windermere
SSE : Alcock Tarn
 S : Esthwaite Water
SSW : Coniston Water
SSW : Grasmere
WSW : Easedale Tarn

ASCENT FROM GRASMERE

Use the lane alongside the Swan Hotel: the second turning on the right leads to a track alongside Greenhead Gill. At the gate turn left: an overgrown path winds round the steep slope ahead between walls. When the open fell is reached incline left to the prominent rocky summit.

THE SUMMIT

from the west

The break in the continuity of the fall along the shoulder is so slight that it is not easy to define the summit exactly; there is no cairn. The height 1652', a survey triangulation point, may well be a big embedded boulder on the highest part of the rocky extremity. The small crags around the summit offer practice for embryo climbers whose main concern is not to drop too far if they fall.

DESCENTS : To find the Grasmere path, aim directly for Alcock Tarn. In mist, any way down is safe after the initial crags are left behind, but unless the path can be found the thick bracken will prove an abomination.

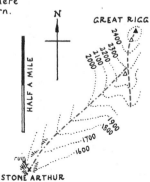

N

GREAT RIGG

HALF A MILE

2400
2300
2200
2100
2000

1900
1800
1700
1600

ruin

STONE ARTHUR

RIDGE ROUTE

To GREAT RIGG, 2513'
1¼ miles : NE then N
Easy climbing all the way
Follow the shoulder upwards;
when it widens and becomes
altogether grassy incline right
to the ridge. Safe in mist.

Stybarrow Dodd 2770'

from Brown Crag

Dockray

▲ GREAT DODD

STYBARROW
▲ DODD

Stanah
Thirlspot

Glencoyne

▲ RAISE

Glenridding

▲ HELVELLYN

MILES
0   1   2   3   4

NATURAL FEATURES

Stybarrow Dodd is the first of the group of fells north of the Sticks Pass and it sets the pattern for them all: sweeping grassy slopes, easy walking for the traveller who likes to count his miles but rather wearisome for those who prefer to see rock in the landscape. Rock is so rare that the slightest roughnesses get undeserved identification on most maps, either by distinctive name or extravagant hachures: thus Deepdale Crag is hardly more than a short stony slope. Stybarrow Dodd sends out a long eastern spur that rises to a minor height, Green Side (which, incidentally, gave its name to the lead mine in nearby Glenridding) before falling steeply to Glencoyne; on Green Side there are both crags and dangerous quarries, now disused.

Stybarrow Dodd's one proud distinction is that on its slopes it carries the well-known path over Sticks Pass throughout most of its length. Far more people ascend the slopes of Stybarrow Dodd than reach its summit!

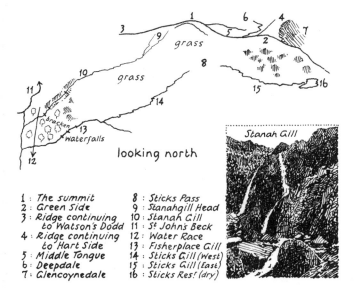

looking north

Stanah Gill

1 : The summit
2 : Green Side
3 : Ridge continuing to Watson's Dodd
4 : Ridge continuing to Hart Side
5 : Middle Tongue
6 : Deepdale
7 : Glencoynedale
8 : Sticks Pass
9 : Stanahgill Head
10 : Stanah Gill
11 : St John's Beck
12 : Water Race
13 : Fisherplace Gill
14 : Sticks Gill (West)
15 : Sticks Gill (East)
16 : Sticks Res! (dry)

MAP

ONE MILE

A path follows the intake wall from Stanah to
Thirlspot. Where it crosses Fisherplace Gill
there is a delightful wooden footbridge
with a perfect view of the beck
and its waterfalls.

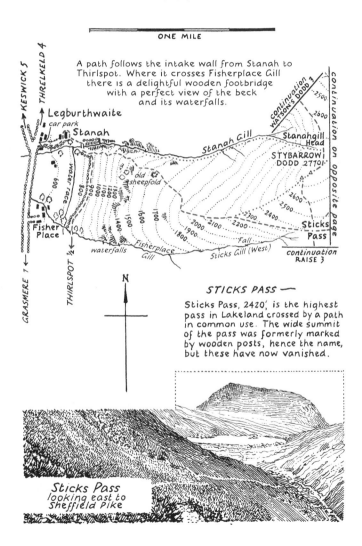

*Sticks Pass
looking east to
Sheffield Pike*

STICKS PASS —

Sticks Pass, 2420′, is the highest
pass in Lakeland crossed by a path
in common use. The wide summit
of the pass was formerly marked
by wooden posts, hence the name,
but these have now vanished.

MAP

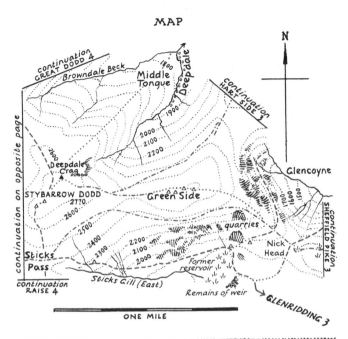

continuation GREAT DODD 4

Browndale Beck

Middle Tongue

1800

Deepdale

continuation HART SIDE 3

N

continuation on opposite page

2600

Deepdale Crag

2000
1900
2100
2200

Glencoyne

1600
1700
1500

STYBARROW DODD
2770

Green Side

2600

quarries

continuation SHEFFIELD PIKE 3

2500

2400
2300

2200
2100
2000

Nick Head

Sticks
Pass

continuation RAISE 4

Sticks Gill (East)

Former reservoir

Remains of weir

GLENRIDDING 3

ONE MILE

Ullswater
from the east slope of Green Side

ASCENT FROM STANAH
2300 feet of ascent : 2½ miles

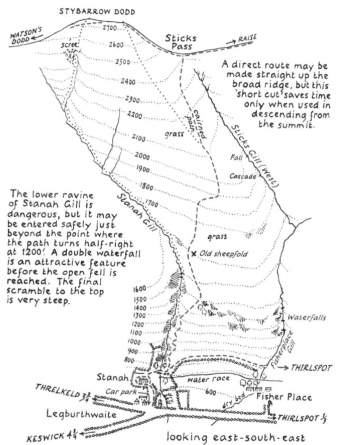

STYBARROW DODD

WATSON'S DODD

scree

2700
2600
2500
2400
2300
2200
2100
2000
1900
1800
1700

Sticks Pass → RAISE

A direct route may be made straight up the broad ridge, but this 'short cut' saves time only when used in descending from the summit.

cairned path

grass

Sticks Gill (west)

Fall

Cascade

Stanah Gill

The lower ravine of Stanah Gill is dangerous, but it may be entered safely just beyond the point where the path turns half-right at 1200! A double waterfall is an attractive feature before the open fell is reached. The final scramble to the top is very steep.

grass

✕ Old sheepfold

1600
1500
1400
1300
1200
1100
1000
900
800

Waterfalls

Fisherplace Gill

→ THIRLSPOT

Stanah

Car park

water race

600

Fisher Place

THRELKELD 3¾

Legburthwaite

dry bed

THIRLSPOT ⅓

KESWICK 4¼ ←

looking east-south-east

Conveniently, the path to Sticks Pass climbs the slopes of Stybarrow Dodd, the summit being easily gained from the top of the pass. Stanah Gill is a rough alternative, affording some relief from the dull grassiness of the path.

ASCENT FROM DOCKRAY
1900 feet of ascent : 5½ miles

STYBARROW DODD

The ascent from
Dockray is not
recommended in
bad weather

WATSON'S DODD →

Deepdale
Crag

2500
2400
2300
2200
2100

GREAT
DODD

Green
Side

HART SIDE

Middle
Tongue

sheepfold

2300

Scot Crag

Deepdale

1900
1800
1700
1600
1500

caves

2200

2100

2000

1900

1800

Coegill Beck

1400

Glencoyne Beck

sheepfold

Little Aira Beck

1700

1600

water
works

Here
the keen
camera
enthusiast
will suffer a
paroxysm
of enthusiasm

Brown
Hills

1800

Swineside
Knott

Watermillock
Common

1500

1400

Dowthwaite
head
(See Great
Dodd 5)

1700

1600

Common
Fell

Glencoyne Park

1400
1300
1200
1100

DOCKRAY 2

Aira Beck

Swineside Knott
is the best
viewpoint for
Ullswater

1200
Round
How

There is no path
at first over the
Common, but one is
soon picked up
following a stream.

DOWTHWAITEHEAD 2

Dockray

looking
west·south·west

ULLSWATER
1¼

TROUTBECK 3 →

parking place

There is all the difference in the world between the
two routes depicted. The direct way up, by Deepdale,
is dreary and depressing; that by the Brown Hills is
(after a dull start) a splendid high·level route, with
excellent views of Ullswater below.

THE SUMMIT

When this book was first published there was no spot height on Stybarrow Dodd and the author suggested that walkers should pass their time on the summit estimating its altitude by this method:

The usually-accepted top is the upright slate slab at the south-western end, (2756'), but there is higher ground 300 yards north-east, indicated by a very loose (at the time of writing!) estate-boundary iron post. That it *is* higher is easily proved: from here, the slate slab at 2756' is seen to cover a part of Esk Pike, 9½ miles away, at about 2400'; therefore the view is *downward*. Q.E.D.
The altitude of the highest point can be roughly decided mathematically. It will be noted that the summit of Raise (2889', 7 furlongs) is directly below the summit of Helvellyn (3080' say, 18 furlongs). The walker didn't climb up here to do sums, and is not likely to challenge the statement that the altitude may, from the data, be calculated at 2770' approximately.

Today no such complex calculations are necessary. The 2½" Ordnance Survey map gives the altitude of the highest point as 843 metres (2766'), which is remarkably close to the author's estimate.
On the highest point there is now a large cairn which incorporates the slate slab. The iron post has gone.

DESCENTS:
All ways off are obvious in clear weather. Think twice before dropping down into Deepdale. *In bad conditions aim south for Sticks Pass.*

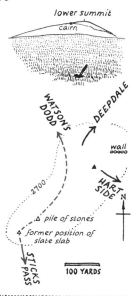

RIDGE ROUTE

To RAISE, 2897': 1 mile: SW then S
Depression at 2420' (Sticks Pass)
470 feet of ascent
An easy walk, mostly on grass. Safe in mist.
From the south-west top, descend south to cross Sticks Pass at its highest point. The long facing slope of Raise becomes stony towards the summit

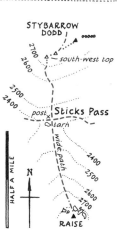

RIDGE ROUTES

To WATSON'S DODD, 2589': ⅔ mile : NW
Depression slight : Ascent negligible
A very easy stroll.
Safe in mist.

A short distance beyond the tarn the path divides into three, the left fork slightly ascending across the flat plateau to the summit-cairn. Beware of marshy ground.

To HART SIDE, 2481' : 1½ miles : E then NE
Depressions at 2525' and 2250' : 300 feet of ascent.
An easy walk on grass. Not recommended in mist.

Descend east, leaving the wall well to the left, to the obvious ridge rising gently to Green Side. Skirt the cairns there and aim directly for Hart Side ahead. Alternatively, bear left in the depression onto the path that skirts Green Side to the north.

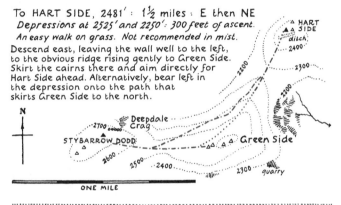

To SHEFFIELD PIKE, 2215' : 2 miles : E then SE and E
Depressions at 2525' and 1925' : 400 feet of ascent
An easy walk. Not recommended in mist.

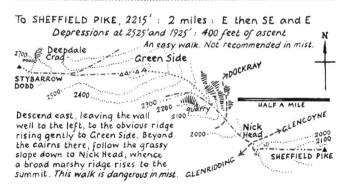

Descend east, leaving the wall well to the left, to the obvious ridge rising gently to Green Side. Beyond the cairns there, follow the grassy slope down to Nick Head, whence a broad marshy ridge rises to the summit. *This walk is dangerous in mist.*

THE VIEW

An extensive and excellent panorama
is seen above a dull and dreary foreground

Principal Fells

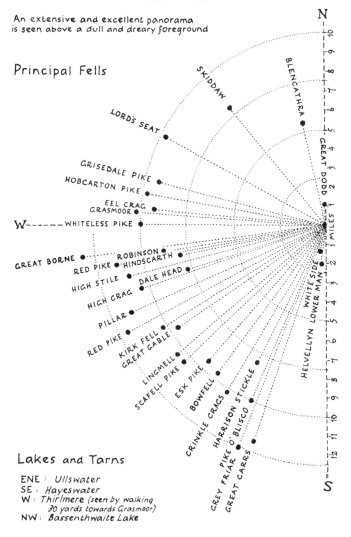

Lakes and Tarns

ENE : Ullswater
SE : Hayeswater
W : Thirlmere (seen by walking
30 yards towards Grasmoor)
NW : Bassenthwaite Lake

THE VIEW

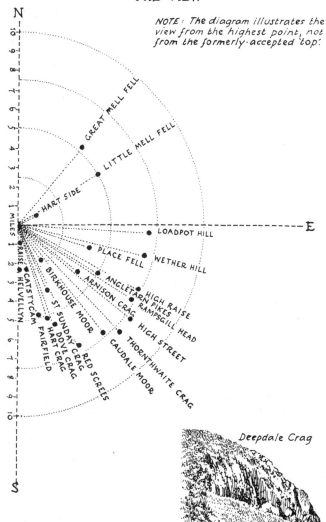

NOTE: The diagram illustrates the view from the highest point, not from the formerly-accepted 'top'.

N
10
9
8
7
6
5
4
3
2
1
MILES
1
2
3
4
5
6
7
8
9
10
S

E

GREAT MELL FELL
LITTLE MELL FELL
HART SIDE
LOADPOT HILL
PLACE FELL
WETHER HILL
HIGH RAISE
ANGLETARN PIKES
ARNISON CRAG
RAMPSGILL HEAD
HIGH STREET
BIRKHOUSE MOOR
ST SUNDAY CRAG
DOVE CRAG
HART CRAG
FAIRFIELD
RED SCREES
THORNTHWAITE CRAG
CAUDALE MOOR
CATSTYCAM
HELVELLYN
RAISE

Deepdale Crag

Watson's Dodd 2589'

▲ GREAT DODD
▲ WATSON'S DODD
● Legburthwaite
● Thirlspot

▲ HELVELLYN

MILES
0 1 2 3 4

from Smaithwaite

NATURAL FEATURES

Whoever Mr. Watson may have been, it is a very odd Dodd that has been selected to perpetuate his name. A separate fell it is undoubtedly, with boundaries unusually sharply defined on north and south by deep ravines, but although it conforms to normal mountain structure on three sides — west, north and south — it has no eastern flanks at all: the slope going down east to Deepdale from the summit-plateau is bisected by a stream that clearly divides Great Dodd and Stybarrow Dodd, and Watson's Dodd cannot stake a claim to any land on this side. In other respects the fell is normal, taking the form of a steepsided ridge, mainly grass with a fringe of crag. With Great Dodd it shares ownership of a very fine ravine, the little-known Mill Gill, but its especial pride and joy is the Castle Rock of Triermain, an imposing and familiar object overlooking the Vale of St John.

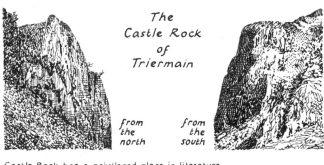

The Castle Rock of Triermain

from the north

from the south

Castle Rock has a privileged place in literature. Sir Walter Scott selected it as the principal scene for "The Bridal of Triermain"

"....midmost of the vale, a mound
Arose, with airy turrets crown'd .....
And mighty keep and tower;"

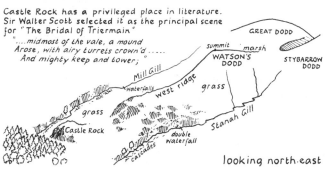

looking north-east

MAP

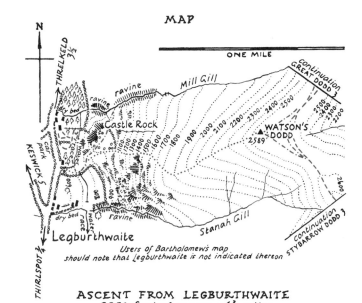

ONE MILE

Users of Bartholomew's map
should note that Legburthwaite is not indicated thereon

ASCENT FROM LEGBURTHWAITE
2050 feet of ascent : 1¼ miles

A path from the
car park to the
road comes out
opposite the gate
giving access to
Castle Rock.

This ascent
promises well, but
deteriorates into a trudge

looking east

THE SUMMIT

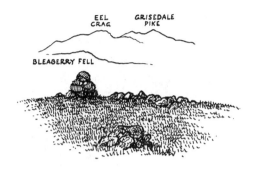

   A few big stones adorn the highest point, at the western end of
the flat triangular top, and they look strangely alien just there
in the universal grassiness of the surroundings, as though they
had been carried there. (Maybe Mr. Watson undertook this task:
if so, it is fitting that the fell should bear his name!). There is a
suggestion of history in these hoary stones.

DESCENTS : The quickest way down to civilisation is by the west
ridge, which commences immediately below the cairn. After half
a mile, when the ground becomes rough, incline right to avoid
crags ahead and aim for the south corner of the wall behind
Castle Rock. *In mist*, use the same route: the ridge is fairly well
defined, but if in doubt incline right rather than left. Avoid
getting into Mill Gill or Stanah Gill, both of which are dangerous.

RIDGE ROUTES

To GREAT DODD, 2812' : ¾ mile : NE
Depression imperceptible: 250 feet of ascent
An easy walk on grass. Safe but confusing in mist.
The path starts indistinctly. It doesn't merge
with the path from Stybarrow Dodd to Great
Dodd, but ends a short distance from it.

To STYBARROW DODD, 2770' :
      ⅔ mile : SE
Depression slight: 200 feet of ascent
An easy walk on grass. Safe in mist.
A small tarn that often dries up is the
only feature. A faint path becomes
clearer at the depression. There is a
cairn on the highest point, near a wall.

Castle Rock and Mill Gill

THE VIEW

The western half of the view is excellent, the eastern half very disappointing indeed.

Principal Fells

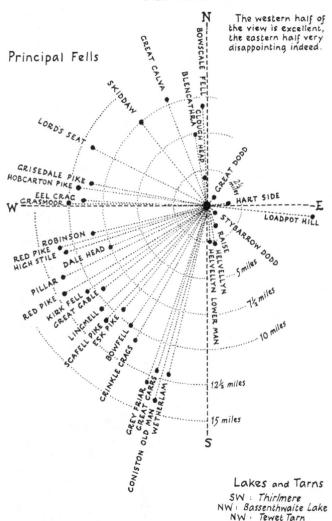

Lakes and Tarns

SW : *Thirlmere*
NW : *Bassenthwaite Lake*
NW : *Tewet Tarn*

White Side

2832'

— a name of convenience.
The summit is strictly nameless,
White Side being the west slope
below the top (probably so-called
from splashes of quartz on many
of the stones).

▲ GREAT DODD

Thirlspot

RAISE ▲   Glenridding

▲ WHITE SIDE

▲ CATSTYCAM

▲ HELVELLYN

• Wythburn

MILES
0   1   2   3   4

from Catstycam

NATURAL FEATURES

Although White Side presents an intimidating wall of low crags to travellers on the road at Thirlspot its upper slopes on this western side are docile enough, being wholly of grass at easy gradients: two paths to Helvellyn cross this flank. Very different is the eastern face, which falls sharply and steeply in crag and scree to the silent recesses of the wild upper Glenridding valley.

The summit is no more than a big grassy mound on the high ridge running northwards from Helvellyn and it rises only slightly above the general level of the ridge.

Skiers and sheep share a high regard for White Side.

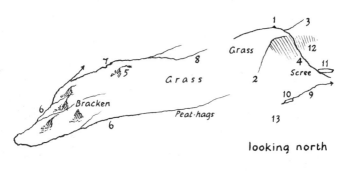

looking north

1: The summit
2: Ridge continuing to Helvellyn Lower Man
3: Ridge continuing to Raise
4: The east ridge
5: Brown Crag
6: Helvellyn Gill
7: Fisherplace Gill
8: Brund Gill
9: Glenridding Beck
10: Tarn in Brown Cove
11: Keppelcove Tarn (dry)
12: Keppel Cove
13: Brown Cove

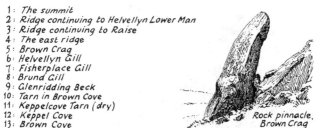

Rock pinnacle,
Brown Crag

The habit of the west-flowing streams of White Side is interesting. It seems natural that they should feed Thirlmere, but a strip of higher ground alongside the lake turns them north into the outflow, St John's Beck. This perversity of nature has been corrected by the Manchester engineers, who have constructed a water race along the base of the fell to collect the water and divert it south into Thirlmere.

MAP

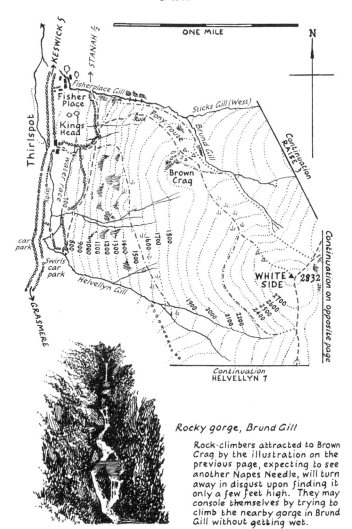

ONE MILE

N

Thirlspot

KESWICK 5

STANAH ½

Fisherplace Gill

Fisher Place

Kings Head

water race

car park

Swirls car park

Helvellyn Gill

GRASMERE

Tony's route

Ruin

Sticks Gill (West)

Brund Gill

Brown Crag

Continuation RAISE 3

Continuation on opposite page

WHITE SIDE ▲ 2832

800 900 1000 1100 1200 1300 1400 1500 1600 1700

1900 2000 2100 2200 2300 2400 2500 2600 2700

Continuation HELVELLYN 7

Rocky gorge, Brund Gill

Rock-climbers attracted to Brown Crag by the illustration on the previous page, expecting to see another Napes Needle, will turn away in disgust upon finding it only a few feet high. They may console themselves by trying to climb the nearby gorge in Brund Gill without getting wet.

Waterfalls in Fisherplace Gill

MAP

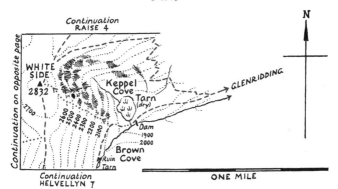

Continuation
RAISE 4

Continuation on opposite page

WHITE
SIDE
▲
2832

2700

2600
2500
2400
2300
2200
2100
2000

Keppel
Cove
Tarn
(dry)

Dam
1900
2000

Brown
Cove

Ruin
Tarn

GLENRIDDING

N

Continuation
HELVELLYN 7

ONE MILE

Tarn in Brown Cove

ASCENT FROM THIRLSPOT
2300 feet of ascent : 2½ miles

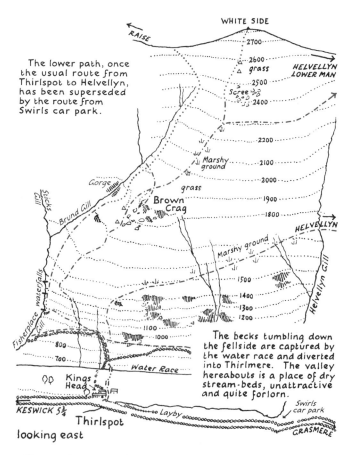

WHITE SIDE

RAISE

2700

HELVELLYN
LOWER MAN

2600
grass

2500

Scree

2400

2200

Marshy
ground

2100

2000

grass

Gorge

1900

Brown
Crag

1800

HELVELLYN

Sticks Gill

Brund Gill

Marshy ground

1500

Helvellyn Gill

1400

1300

1200

Fisherplace Gill

waterfalls

1100

1000

800

700

Water Race

Kings
Head

KESWICK 5¾

Thirlspot

Layby

Swirls
car park

GRASMERE

looking east

The lower path, once the usual route from Thirlspot to Helvellyn, has been superseded by the route from Swirls car park.

The becks tumbling down the fellside are captured by the water race and diverted into Thirlmere. The valley hereabouts is a place of dry stream-beds, unattractive and quite forlorn.

Two paths cross the western flank of White Side above Thirlspot. They lead to Helvellyn, but the upper one is conveniently placed for the ascent of White Side: it is an easy climb on grass after initial steepness.

ASCENT FROM GLENRIDDING
2400 feet of ascent : 4 miles from Glenridding village

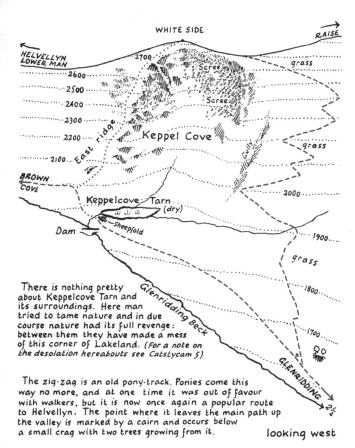

WHITE SIDE

RAISE

HELVELLYN
LOWER MAN

2700

Scree

grass

2600

2500

2400

Scree

2300

2200

Keppel Cove

Gully

grass

2100

East ridge

BROWN
COVE

2000

Keppelcove · Tarn
(dry)

Dam

Sheepfold

1900

grass

1800

Glenridding Beck

There is nothing pretty
about Keppelcove Tarn and
its surroundings. Here man
tried to tame nature and in due
course nature had its full revenge:
between them they have made a mess
of this corner of Lakeland. *(For a note on
the desolation hereabouts see Catstycam 5)*

1700

GLENRIDDING

2½

The zig·zag is an old pony·track. Ponies come this
way no more, and at one time it was out of favour
with walkers, but it is now once again a popular route
to Helvellyn. The point where it leaves the main path up
the valley is marked by a cairn and occurs below
a small crag with two trees growing from it.

looking west

There are few high fells more easily climbed than White
Side if the zig·zag path from Glenridding is used.   The
other route shown, by the east ridge, is very different; it
is pathless, steep and stony, but not difficult.

THE SUMMIT

The summit of White Side is marked by a large cairn and a wind shelter facing north-west, with grassy slopes descending gently away on all sides, although north-eastwards the ground falls away sharply around the rim of Keppel Cove.

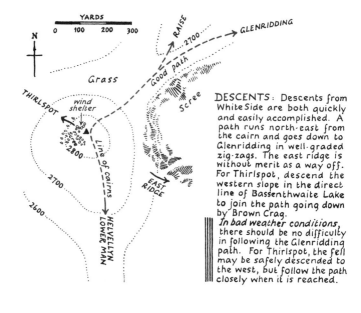

DESCENTS: Descents from White Side are both quickly and easily accomplished. A path runs north-east from the cairn and goes down to Glenridding in well-graded zig-zags. The east ridge is without merit as a way off. For Thirlspot, descend the western slope in the direct line of Bassenthwaite Lake to join the path going down by Brown Crag.

In bad weather conditions, there should be no difficulty in following the Glenridding path. For Thirlspot, the fell may be safely descended to the west, but follow the path closely when it is reached.

THE VIEW

Helvellyn shuts out the distant scene southwards, but in all other directions the panorama is very good, especially to the west. The best picture is provided by Skiddaw, with Bassenthwaite Lake at its foot.

Principal Fells

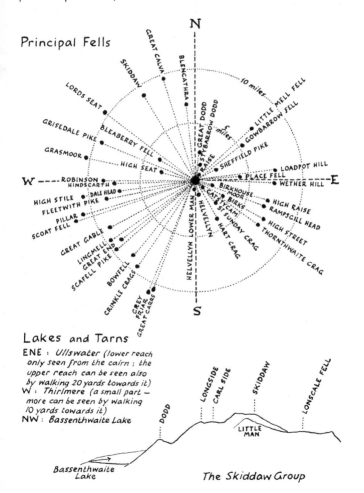

Lakes and Tarns

ENE : *Ullswater (lower reach only seen from the cairn ; the upper reach can be seen also by walking 20 yards towards it)*
W : *Thirlmere (a small part — more can be seen by walking 10 yards towards it)*
NW : *Bassenthwaite Lake*

The Skiddaw Group

RIDGE ROUTES

To HELVELLYN LOWER MAN, 3033' : 1 mile : S

Depression at 2600'
450 feet of ascent

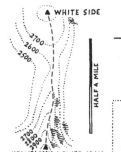

A grassy descent and a long stony climb.
Easy. Safe in mist.

Follow the line of cairns: a fair path leads down to the depression and it continues distinctly up the long ridge ahead, becoming very loose and stony.

To RAISE, 2897'
¾ mile : NE
Depression at 2650'
250 feet of ascent
Easy walking on grass.
Safe in mist.

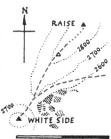

A good path leads down to the depression (where a branch descends to Glenridding). Strike up the ridge ahead, following a wide ribbon of gravel, and after reaching a cairn cross the level plateau to the stony summit.

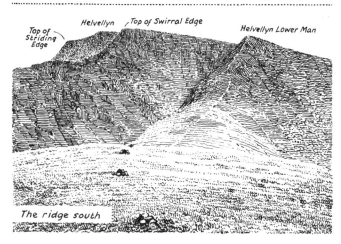

The ridge south

The East Ridge
(In the foreground, the burst
banks of Keppelcove Tarn)

THE EASTERN FELLS
Some Personal Notes
in conclusion

I suppose it might be said, to add impressiveness to the whole thing, that this book has been twenty years in the making, for it is so long, and more, since I first came from a smoky mill-town (forgive me, Blackburn!) and beheld, from Orrest Head, a scene of great loveliness, a fascinating paradise, Lakeland's mountains and trees and water. That was the first time I had looked upon beauty, or imagined it, even. Afterwards I went often, whenever I could, and always my eyes were lifted to the hills. I was to find then, and it has been so ever since, a spiritual and physical satisfaction in climbing mountains — and a tranquil mind upon reaching their summits, as though I had escaped from the disappointments and unkindnesses of life and emerged above them into a new world, a better world.

But that is by the way. In those early Lakeland days I served my apprenticeship faithfully, learning all the time. At first, the hills were frightening, moody giants, and I a timid Gulliver, but very gradually through the years we became acquaintances and much later firm friends.

In due course I came to live within sight of the hills, and I was well content. If I could not be climbing, I was happy to sit idly and dream of them, serenely. Then came a restlessness and the feeling that it was not enough to take their gifts and do nothing in return. I must dedicate something of myself, the best part of me, to them. I started to write about them, and to draw pictures of them. Doing these things, I found they were still giving and I still receiving, for a great pleasure filled me when I was so engaged — I had found a new way of escape to them and from all else less worth while.

Thus it comes about that I have written this book. Not for material gain, welcome though that would be (you see I have not escaped entirely!); not for the benefit of my contemporaries, though if it brings them also to the hills I shall be well pleased; certainly not for posterity, about which I can work up no enthusiasm at all. No, this book has been written, carefully and with infinite patience, for my own pleasure and because it has seemed to bring the hills to my own fireside. If it has merit, it is because the hills have merit.

I started the book determined that everything in it should be perfect, with the consequence that I spent the first six months filling wastepaper baskets. Only then did I accept what I should have known and acknowledged from the start — that nothing created by man is perfect, or can hope to be; and having thus consoled and cheered my hurt conceit I got along like a house on fire. So let me be the first to say it: this book is full of imperfections. But let me dare also to say that (apart from many minor blemishes of which I am already deeply conscious and have no wish to be reminded) it is free from inaccuracies.

The group of fells I have named the Eastern Fells are old favourites, not quite as exciting as the Scafell heights, perhaps, but enjoyable territory for the walker. They are most conveniently climbed from the west, which is a pity, for the finest approaches are from the Patterdale valley to the east. The walking is easy for the most part; very easy along the main watershed. The coves below the summits eastwards are a feature of these hills: rarely visited, they are very impressive in their craggy surroundings. Exploration also reveals many interesting evidences of old and abandoned industries — quarries, mines, aqueducts, disused paths. Somebody should write a geographical history of these enterprises before all records are lost.

Some of my experiences during many solitary wanderings while collecting information for this book would be worth the telling, but I preserve the memories for the time when I can no longer climb. One, however, returns insistently to mind...... I remember a sunny day in the wilderness of Ruthwaite Cove: I lay idly on the warm rocks alongside Hard Tarn, with desolation everywhere but in my heart, where was peace. The air was still; there was no sound, and nothing in view but the shattered confusion of rocks all around. I might have been the last man in a dead world. A tiny splash drew my gaze to the crystal-clear depths of the tarn .... a newt was swimming there, just beneath the surface. I watched it for a long time. And I fell to wondering.......

wondering about it, and its mission as it circled the smooth waters, and the purpose of its life — and mine. A trivial thing to remember, maybe, yet I do. I often think of that small creature, a speck of life in the immensity of desolation in which it had its being.

It is a remarkable thing, now that I come to think of it, that I still set forth for a day on the hills with the eagerness I felt when they were new to me. So it is that I have thoroughly enjoyed my walks whilst this book has been in preparation, much more so because I have walked with a purpose. Yet recently my gaze has been wandering more and more from the path, and away to the fells east of Kirkstone — my next area of exploration.

So, although I take my leave of the Eastern Fells with very real regret, as one parts from good friends, I look forward to equally happy days on the Far Eastern Fells. When this last sentence is written Book One will be finished, and in the same moment Book Two will take its place in my thoughts.

Christmas, 1954   AW.

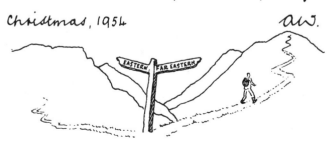